Who Runs the E

Robert Skidelsky • Nan Craig
Editors

Who Runs the Economy?

The Role of Power in Economics

Editors
Robert Skidelsky
University of Warwick
Warwickshire, United Kingdom

Nan Craig
Centre for Global Studies
London, United Kingdom

ISBN 978-1-137-58018-4 (hardback)   ISBN 978-1-137-58019-1 (paperback)
ISBN 978-1-137-58017-7 (eBook)
DOI 10.1057/978-1-137-58017-7

Library of Congress Control Number: 2016951095

Cover illustration: © Textures and backgrounds / Alamy Stock Photo

Printed on acid-free paper

This Palgrave Macmillan imprint is published by Springer Nature
The registered company is Macmillan Publishers Ltd. London

Preface and Acknowledgments

The symposium 'Power and Economics' took place over four sessions in London on 23 March 2015. Transcripts were made of the presentations and discussions. The following essays arose from the presentations given, and we have tried to give a sense of the discussion in our Introduction.

We would like to thank the House of Lords for making the conference room available and providing refreshments; the Centre for Global Studies, which made the symposium financially possible; Laurie Laybourn-Langton for organising the event; Rachel Sangster, Laura Pacey, and Gemma Leigh at Palgrave Macmillan; Ubiqus, for transcription services; and of course all those who attended, as speakers or as discussants.

Robert Skidelsky
Nan Craig

Contents

Notes on Contributors

Roger Backhouse is a professor of History and Philosophy of Economics at the Department of Economics, University of Birmingham and Erasmus University Rotterdam. His publications include a book on John Maynard Keynes, and the history of the social sciences since 1945, and, with Mauro Boianovsky, *Transforming Modern Macroeconomics: Exploring Disequilibrium Microfoundations, 1956–2003* (2013).

Nancy Cartwright is a professor of Philosophy at the Department of Philosophy, University of Durham and at the University of California, San Diego. Her publications include *How the Laws of Physics Lie* (1983) and *The Dappled World: A Study of the Boundaries of Science* (1999).

Nan Craig is Programme Director at the Centre for Global Studies. She studied Politics and International Studies at the University of Warwick and Global Politics at the London School of Economics.

John B. Davis is a professor in the Department of Economics at Marquette University and Amsterdam School of Economics at the University of Amsterdam. He is the author of *Keynes's Philosophical Development* (1994), *The Theory of the Individual in Economics* (2003), and *Individuals and Identity in Economics* (2011).

James Galbraith is Lloyd M. Bentsen Jr. Chair in Government/Business Relations and professor of Government in the Lyndon B. Johnson School of Public Affairs at the University of Texas at Austin. His publications include

Inequality and Instability: A Study of the World Economy Just Before the Great Crisis (2012) and *The End of Normal: The Great Crisis and the Future of Growth* (2014).

Norbert Haering is a correspondent for Handelsblatt, and co-director of the World Economics Association. He is the author, with Niall Douglas, of *Economists and the Powerful* (2013).

Jonathan Hearn is a senior lecturer in Sociology in the School of Social and Political Science at the University of Edinburgh, UK. He is the author of *Claiming Scotland: National Identity and Liberal Culture* (2000), *Rethinking Nationalism: A Critical Introduction* (2006), and *Theorizing Power* (2012).

Anthony Heath is a professor of Sociology at the Centre for Social Investigation, Nuffield College, Oxford. His books include *The Political Integration of Ethnic Minorities in Britain* (2013) and *Unequal Attainments: Ethnic Educational Inequalities in Ten Western Countries* (2014).

Ben Jackson is associate professor of Modern History in the Department of History at Oxford University and a Fellow of University College. He is the author of *Equality and the British Left* (2007) and the co-editor, with Robert Saunders, of *Making Thatcher's Britain* (2012).

Steven Lukes is a professor of Sociology in the Department of Sociology at New York University, USA. He has written many books about political and social theory, including the seminal *Power: A Radical View* (1974) and also *Emile Durkheim: His Life and Work* (1975).

Thomas Palley is an economist living in Washington DC. He was formerly chief economist with the US-China Economic and Security Review Commission, Director of the Open Society Institute's Globalization Reform Project, and Assistant Director of Public Policy at the AFL-CIO. His books include *Plenty of Nothing: The Downsizing of the American Dream and* the *Case for Structural Keynesianism* (1998).

Robert Skidelsky is emeritus professor of Political Economy in the Department of Economics at Warwick University. His publications include a three-volume biography of John Maynard Keynes (1983, 1992, 2000); *Keynes: The Return of the Master* (2010); with Edward Skidelsky, *How Much is Enough? The Love of Money and the Case for the Good Life* (2012); and most recently *Britain in the 20th Century: A Success?* (2014). He is editor of *The Essential Keynes* (2015).

Daniel Stedman Jones is a barrister practising in London, and the author of *Masters of the Universe: Hayek, Friedman, and the Birth of Neoliberal Politics* (2012).

Adair Turner is chairman of the Institute for New Economic Thinking and former chairman of the Financial Services Authority. He is the author of *Economics after the Crisis* (2012) and most recently, *Between Debt and the Devil* (2015).

Lucas Zeise is a financial columnist for the *Financial Times Deutschland*. His most recent book is *Geld—der vertrackte Kern des Kapitalismus* (2012).

List of Figures

List of Tables

1

Introduction

Robert Skidelsky and Nan Craig

The following essays are based on talks given at a symposium on 'Power and Economics' organised by the Centre for Global Studies in March 2015. Our symposium took as its starting point the thought of how little change the Greater Recession had brought about in the system of ideas, institutions, and policies which preceded the economic collapse of 2008. This led us to consider the relationship between economic ideas and power. It is not entirely absent; as Thomas Palley pointed out, economists discuss market power, bargaining power, and so on. However, this is a discussion within the discipline. It fails to explore the reciprocal connections between economic ideas and politics: the political power of economic ideas on the one side, and the influence of power structures on economic thought on the other. Was it correct to say, as Keynes famously did, that 'the power of vested interests is vastly exaggerated compared with gradual

R. Skidelsky (✉)
University of Warwick, Warwickshire, UK

N. Craig
Centre for Global Studies, London, UK

© The Editor(s) (if applicable) and The Author(s) 2016   **1**
R. Skidelsky, N. Craig (eds.), *Who Runs the Economy?*,
DOI 10.1057/978-1-137-58017-7_1

encroachment of ideas', that 'soon or late, it is ideas, not vested interests, which are dangerous for good or evil'.[1] Or was Marx right to regard economics as the ideology of the triumphant bourgeoisie? A key conclusion of the discussion was that power is under-theorised in economics. This was a debate that we returned to many times over the day: to what extent are economists ignoring power, or, at the very least, ignoring major facets of power—both their own power and the power dynamics within the social world they study? These elements overlap, as Nancy Cartwright described, through looping effects and self-fulfilling prophecies, as economic theories are picked up by the financial and policy worlds. The supposedly neutral discipline of economics does not simply describe human behaviour but, in fact, shapes it.

We began with presentations from Steven Lukes and Jonathan Hearn, detailing the basic dynamics of economics and power. Then, the superstructure of economics, with Norbert Häring of *Handelsblatt* and Lucas Zeise. Nancy Cartwright and John Bryan Davis completed the theoretical component of the day with presentations on economics as a science, including how power affects debates within economics.

Steven Lukes gave a triadic view of power—that, in addition to power over decision-making and power over agenda-setting, there exists a third type of power, as described by J. K. Galbraith in his book *The Anatomy of Power*, which is power of conditioning—the power to shape others' interests and preferences, so that they are not even aware of their 'real' interests. This takes preferences not as exogenously given, but as shaped. In some cases, objectively observable harms do not develop into grievances.

Jonathan Hearn noted that a discussion of this third form of power is necessarily different from the first two, because it is 'fundamentally conceived as a critique of harm'. The evidence for this third form of power is not in the behaviour of dominant actors, but in the harm done to the dominated—that is, the difference between their true interests and their preferences.

He also argued that intention is hard to discern here or, rather, that intention and action can be complex, and that beliefs 'can be both prevalent and under question at the same time'—for instance, in the case Steven Lukes raised of the repeal of the California estate tax, or 'death tax', where voters voted clearly against their own interests.

---

[1] Keynes, J. M. 'The General Theory of Employment, Interest and Money', (1936), p.384.

In the following discussion, Anthony Giddens questioned whether this definition of power was analytically clear enough to be useful:

> Power is everywhere and nowhere. It is elusive, so you need some kind of definition [...] to my mind the Parsonian idea—the two forms of power, there is power as capability and there is power as power over people—is not a bad starting point.

He added, 'You could argue neoclassical economic theory is kind of in denial of power; it portrays the economy as if power were not there.' Yuan Yang agreed that

> Neoclassical economics is both an exercise of discursive power, but also ignores many of the problems to do with that power. [...] It seems to me that many economists have an allergy to dealing with ethical philosophy, which means that when you get in normative concepts such as benefits, interests and freedom, which came up early in both your presentations, that is the point at which many neoclassical economists will switch off and say, "This is a job for the philosophers and not for us." That means that many economists spend their careers rationalising forms of power.

Thomas Palley noted, 'There is a very old concept called false consciousness, and it seems that is what we are talking about here [...] that is how I have always thought of Galbraith's conditioned power.' He added,

> False consciousness is a slightly paternalistic concept and it is probably the most difficult political problem: how far can you go to unravel false consciousness? At the worst you end up with Stalin and Mao, and alternatively you end up with the United States that is in total denial about its existence, and maybe that is the neo-liberal era for us.

Andrew Graham added that,

> Of course, it is true that economists talk all the time about market power, and bargaining, but they do not talk about ideology. That is a term that, a bit like false consciousness, has not come back onto the table. [...] The other word we have not yet had is equality. Economists at the moment do not have much to say about the whole massive inequality that has emerged.

In the next session of the day, Norbert Häring laid out a series of shifts in economic thinking and orthodoxy over the centuries, and how these were affected by the needs of powerful interests. The four shifts he described range from the beginning of the industrial revolution in Britain—the first being the shift from protectionism, originally the natural policy to protect nascent British industries, to the promotion of free trade once these industries had become established. The second was in the nineteenth century, with the shift from classical to neoclassical economics, which Häring ascribes to the need to defend against the threat of Marxism. The third came during the 1930s, when the threat of revolution shifted to that of redistribution, with the redefining of economics to the study of the relationship between ends and scarce means. Häring argued that the fourth shift is a continuation of the third, where the dominance of methodological individualism, rational choice theory and public choice theory in economics serves the interests of the few against the possibility of collective decision-making. Finally, he argued it can be more useful to consider who or what is served by a particular idea, than whether that idea is strictly correct or incorrect.

Lucas Zeise, in his discussion of Häring's talk, agreed with his argument that ideas in economics have developed mainly along the lines required for the perpetuation of power by specific interests. He also stressed the importance of the idea of 'superstructure'—the Marxist idea that the 'class system of society is established and stabilised by a superstructure that, on the one hand, is built upon the economy, and on the other, keeps the economy in its class structure, in its capitalist mode'.

In the discussion that followed, Edward Skidelsky opened by pointing out that there was no clear theory to explain why economists needed to justify the ruling class. Adair Turner, in response, argued that it may be traceable to employment prospects, since the growth since the 1970s in the numbers of economists employed in the financial services sector may well make them unlikely to question theories in economics that support the financial sector. Norbert Häring argued that, in his experience of the German university system, there were clear professional advantages to espousing the most conveniently mainstream version of economics—one which is advantageous to the financial sector. In addition, he suggested, even academic economists have to train PhD economists who will go to work outside the academy and are therefore required to teach them ideas that will fit their roles in business. Steven Lukes raised the issue of 'physics envy', which he argued was rife in the social sciences but particularly acute amongst economists. He argued that economics has attempted to produce a 'unified theory', where a universally applicable theory of micro-behaviour—which assumes that preferences are given and exogenous—provides the foundations for macroeconomic thought.

Anthony Giddens reflected on the fact that the unanticipated, non-violent collapse of Marxism and communism in the 1990s may have had an effect in 'liberating a certain version of economics in the west with a triumphalist background', and, second, that there may be more than one layer to the story—'the contest of ideas and their relationship to the real world'. Roger Backhouse, however, stressed the importance of complicating the historical narrative and de-homogenising this account of neoclassical economics—for instance, by acknowledging the shift between the economics of Frank Knight, who wrote extensively on ethics, to that of his pupils Stigler and Becker, who espoused the Chicago school view that it was wrong to question people's tastes or preferences. Jonathan Hearn argued in response that, in fact, the interesting aspect was the homogenising of neoclassicism—why has neoclassical economics taken it as incontestable that markets are sites of perfect competition? David Runciman suggested that, to the contrary, perfect competition is an account of power, but an account that argues advantages to smaller players in the system, and which is suspicious of the state as the one player which is not subject to the disruptive competitive forces of the market. Thomas Palley added to the argument that it was also important that the ruling class should not be considered as homogeneous, either, and that the ruling class can also suffer from their own version of false consciousness—such as in the case of industrial leaders who feel they cannot argue against free trade, despite the damage it does to their own business. Finally, Jonathan Hearn suggested in response to David Runciman that, indeed, economics does not remove power from its argument, so much as naturalise it and fail to question it.

In the third session, we moved on to a discussion of the relationship between science and economics. Nancy Cartwright's presentation touched on two areas: whether economics can be called a science, and also the ways in which it is granted power simply because it is *perceived* as a science, whatever its true attributes. The power of economics rests on several effects, the first being reflexivity—a 'looping' effect in which economic theories are self-fulfilling. Another is the power inherent in the ability to design measures and models—such as in deciding how to measure poverty. Choice of model can highlight or bury issues such as distribution, since no model can describe everything, so, depending on what is left out, important issues can be invisible or inexpressible.

John Davis' presentation expressed a concern that economics is becoming 'essentially a performative science', which could become vulnerable to a collapse similar to that of alchemy and other pseudo-sciences. He argued that this had happened due to the breakdown of economics' 'reflexive practices' as a discipline, including the fixing of a hierarchy of economics journals and departments, and the marginalisation of the methodological and historical aspects of economics, which previously acted as its 'principal forms of scientific self-consciousness'. He further argued that the increasing insularity of economics explained why so many recent advances in the field had come from the introduction of approaches from other social sciences, such as behaviourism from psychology.

Three issues emerged in the discussion that followed. First, the difficulty of testing economics empirically, and whether there is a different possibility of testability in micro- versus macroeconomics. Second, there is the question of whether it is possible, or desirable, to build macroeconomics on micro-foundations. Third, the group discussed the range of techniques or effects through which economics becomes a powerful political tool.

Roger Backhouse asked whether, in fact, the examples that Nancy Cartwright had given of Tony Atkinson's work on inequality and that of Nicholas Stern on climate change, were actually counter-examples to the case John Davis presented for a failure of reflexivity in economics.

Cartwright agreed that they were, in one sense, but that they were also welfare economists of a specific era, whose approach to economics is not likely to continue in a younger generation: 'Welfare economics is not taught at the London School of Economics'. John Davis added that he did not intend to portray economics as monolithic but, rather, point out the failings of 'rational choice [...] as the performative mainstream'.

Anthony Heath argued that the larger problem was the difficulty in properly testing any hypotheses in economics,

That [...] is why economics can get away with it, in a way that medicine cannot. You would not do the sorts of things economists do if you were making decisions in medicine. You would not use instrumental variable methods, for example, when you were deciding on treatment outcomes.

Adair Turner agreed that there are some areas where economics can be tested, and that these tend to produce useful evidence, 'they produce very different results in different areas of economics and, in particular, between some categories of microeconomics, macro and finance'. He argued that as Chairman of the Low Pay Commission, he found research on labour markets and monopsony was helpful, as was the use of behavioural economics to the Pensions Commission. Both of these are areas in which policies can be tested and results observed, to some degree. However, macroeconomic policy is impossible to test in the same way: 'The difficulty with macro is that you cannot run Economy A for the next 10 years in one fashion, Economy B in another fashion and then observe which one performs better.' He added,

What that means is that economics must not migrate solely to try to answer the things that it can answer. We have to be aware that the different degrees by which we can test different propositions can, unless we are careful, drag us towards saying things on micro issues and avoiding some of the most important issues with which economics has to engage.

Andrew Graham argued that, in fact, it was wrong to think that microeconomics was more effective than macroeconomics, adding,

I would like to return to the book by Bernard Williams, *Truth and Truthfulness*.[2] He thinks we can almost always tell whether people are trying to be truth tellers. He does not make the silly mistake of thinking there is such a thing as truth, but he thinks we can tell whether people are trying to do it or not. You can apply that to good historians, economists or physicists. Almost always you would do it by looking at more than one truth-telling story. [...] If I was a truth teller who then looked at microeconomics,

---

[2] Williams (2004).

the assumption that the representative agent is always, everywhere, rational in the economic sense is just obviously not true.

Adair Turner responded that

> I completely agree with you. I said […] that some of micro had been helpful: the empirical parts of micro, the behavioural economics of micro and the bits of micro that explicitly rejected rational expectations and choice, for instance the behavioural stuff that feed into auto-enrolment systems. I completely agree with you that the fundamental problem of macro is that, about 40 years ago, we developed a hypothesis that we had to have micro foundations of macro theory. The micro foundations on which we built it were the most absurd you could ever imagine. I think it reasonable to say that some of micro since then has moved away from those incredibly simplistic foundations, and macro has stuck in a rational expectations world that a lot of the best micro now rejects.

Thomas Palley countered:

> I do not think that the project is wrong. We do need some sort of micro foundation […] What we come back to is the problem that economics has always insisted on neoclassical micro foundations.

He added, 'The concept of pluralism becomes key. It is not pluralism because I like difference or I am a nice guy. I am pluralistic because your hypothesis, which I happen to disagree with, passes the tests that we have right now.'

The afternoon sessions moved on to case studies, first historical and then present-day, with the aim of describing shifts in economic thinking over the twentieth century, and how these had exerted power over policy as well as over 'common sense' or the received wisdom of the period.

Robert Skidelsky argued that the success of Keynesianism in producing full employment over the early part of the twentieth century had induced a form of amnesia that allowed the 'ills of the market' to be forgotten and classical economics to be rehabilitated. An intellectual shift happened over the 1970s and 1980s, including the rise in Schumpeterian ideas and Austrian theory. Second, Keynesianism failed to resolve the Ricardo–Marx problem of wages, and Keynesian governments in the 1970s resorted to inflation as a 'vent for social conflict'. Third, there was a political shift against trade unions, and fourth, the structure of the economy shifted towards the financial sector and service sector. Finally, globalisation has undermined workers' economic power. The consequence is that the social contract of the welfare state has been replaced by access to credit, which was and continues to be inherently unstable.

Roger Backhouse took up the discussion, in the context of the USA, in particular in the 1930s. He argued that although there were close connections, the experiences of Britain and the USA were not the same. Instead of the stagnation in Britain after World War I, the frontier and individualism were important factors for the USA, and there was a massive boom preceding the collapse, so it was possible to think of the Depression as a business cycle gone wrong—that it was a failure of competition due to monopoly and oligopoly. He went on to illustrate this through the activities of the Temporary National Economic Committee (TNEC), which was established in 1938 to study monopoly power. Two of the witnesses called were Keynesian economists Hansen and Currie, who shifted the discussion of the Committee from monopoly power to financial flows. The association of Keynesianism with the TNEC report lead to hostility to Keynesianism because it was associated with a critique or attack on economic power.

The following discussion broadly covered the question of 'balance of powers' in an economy, and whether it can be enough to break up a monopoly of corporate power, or whether it is essential to have other countervailing forces, such as unions. As Jonathan Hearn said, 'I am struck by how much the analytical language in both talks is about "balance of forces", "social balance", "countervailing power" or "concentration of power"'. He went on to compare this with international relations theory, where 'balance of power' is a key concept.

Thomas Palley argued that unions are 'absolutely essential for a social-democratic shared-prosperity society' and that,

I know from economic history of no country that has succeeded in making the transition to a developed economy, such as we know in most of the

OECD countries, without going through a period of mass unionisation. There is no institution, as we have yet come up with, that can accomplish the needed distribution of income for full employment that unions can do.

Nevertheless, he added that unions include political problems and, at least in the UK, are now associated with the excesses of the 1970s, so that making unions relevant and important again is a crucial problem.

Thomas Palley also disagreed with Robert Skidelsky's characterisation of Keynesianism as a theory with an inherent normative element—positing, rather, that Keynes 'provides an organising principle for understanding capitalist economies'. He also argued that Keynesianism in the USA has had its own character, quite different to European Keynesianism, and including a form of military Keynesianism in the 1980s, which is now a plutocratic Keynesianism. Robert Skidelsky responded that Keynesianism was 'a rejection of extremes; it was the idea that you could, through intelligent management, ensure a harmonious and prosperous society and economy working at full employment. There was a social vision there.'

The next session focused on the neo-classical counter-revolution in the twentieth century, beginning with a presentation by Daniel Stedman Jones on the history of neoliberalism, and Ben Jackson on the battle of ideas and the history of think-tanks.

Daniel Stedman Jones described the origins of 'neoliberalism' with Friedrich Hayek and the Mont Pelerin Society, going on to trace its political success across the twentieth century. He outlined three dimensions of neoliberalism that are related to power within economics. First, the critiques of the Chicago and Virginia Schools rewrote the understanding of power, from early liberals' understanding of regulation as enhancing competition to the assumption that government was the problem and should be removed entirely. The second dimension is Hayek's and Friedman's focus on 'the importance of a transatlantic, indeed global, political network and a model of change and the influence of economics on political power'. Third, how economic ideas actually change politics— Do events and changing economic circumstances affect which ideas are successful, as it appeared to have done in the case of neoliberalism?

Ben Jackson's talk focused more closely on the Institute of Economic Affairs (IEA) in Britain and how it attempted to produce and shape 'conventional wisdom'—that is, what could be considered politically feasible. He stressed that it was important not to see this as a pure 'battle of ideas' but, rather, as 'a concerted effort that was sponsored by a sympathetic business elite to disseminate these ideas through an international network of interlocking institutions'. In particular, they struck on the method of influencing the small media and political elite of 1960s and 1970s Britain. He also argued that the influence of heavy-weights such as Hayek and Friedman meant that the success of the IEA could in some way be regarded as the Americanisation of the British political debate.

The discussion afterwards concentrated on how the intellectual debate shifted across the twentieth century—What were the influences? John Kay made the point that many think-tanks in the 1960s and 1970s were funded by corporations—and 'that kind of funding started to disappear as think-tanks proliferated and as shareholder-value rhetoric-spouting companies came to be more aggressive through the 1980s. It looks sinister now in a way that really was not true at the time.' Paul Flather noted that the IEA was keen to influence left-leaning journalists and academics, not only those with an interest in neoliberal ideas. There was an attempt to create a social and intellectual milieu rather than self-consciously to promote specific ideas. Both Daniel Stedman Jones and Ben Jackson agreed that the IEA's aim originally was to create the ability to influence. Ben Jackson added,

> In a way, what the IEA did was create a sense of intellectual community. That was obviously underpinned by a particular vision they had, but they welcomed all sorts of people ... creating a sense of fun and intellectual community and having these very convivial lunches that got people together.

Adair Turner added that 'We cannot separate out the take-off of the IEA and neoclassical ideas ... in particular in the 1970s, from the fact that the prior model was not working'—in that, for instance, Keynesian theories at the time failed to explain stagflation.

Robert Skidelsky suggested that economics tended to be dominated by one major theory after another—is economic pluralism ever truly possible, or is this a Kuhnian model in which one paradigm reigns, only to be replaced by another? Adair Turner argued that, in comparison with physics, for example, the history of economics is always useful and relevant, much in the same way that new modes of art do not permanently supersede older ones: 'We did not say, once the cubists came along, that we could never see the world in a pre-Raphaelite way or, post cubism, we could never see the world in a cubist way. Of course, these are all perspectives that have something to offer.' Nancy Cartwright argued that, in fact, physicists are not intellectually homogenous—that there continue to be debates in the natural sciences, and that one theory does not cleanly supersede another.

Thomas Palley suggested that the culture of different scientific communities, and willingness of some economists and economic departments to tolerate pluralism, could affect shifts in economic ideas: 'You have two communities. If one is tolerant and gives over some of its positions to the other side because it believes in that, and the other is utterly intolerant, the intolerant population inevitably starts to dominate and becomes one hundred percent.'

Steven Lukes pointed out that a historical grounding is assumed in sociology, while this is fading from political science and completely absent from economics, where the emphasis is on ahistorical 'scientific' theories: 'It is interesting to look at economics compared to the other social sciences. It is, it seems to me, bent on unification.'

In the final session of the afternoon, we moved into the present-day to look at how economics and power interact in the modern economy.

Adair Turner discussed the role of economics and power in banking, arguing that macroeconomics entirely missed the significance of the financialization of the economy—in particular, that it depended on a growth in credit that fuelled consumption, not capital investment by business. It also ignored the dangers in the rise in intra-financial system complexity, assuming that spreading risk across the whole system through complicated systems of credit would make the system more resilient, not less. In the liberalisation of the economy, this was partly related to overt lobbying by banks for further liberalisation of finance from the 1970s onwards, but also to the intellectually seductive idea that liberalisation would automatically create better outcomes; 'a confluence of private industry interests and apparently desirable social objectives'.

Following on from this, Thomas Palley gave a presentation on the age of 'market worship' that has developed over the last 40 years, that attributes special standing to financial markets. He argued that the concept of efficient markets, which has guided thinking about finance, should be replaced by the concept of financialization. The latter refers to the process whereby finance exerts increasing influence over the real economy, economic policy and politics. In doing so, it increases income inequality, creates financial fragility and proclivity to economic instability, and generates macroeconomic inefficiency in the form of slower growth. Adopting a financialization perspective generates a dramatically different policy agenda for restoring shared prosperity.

From financialization and the economics of banking, we moved on to how power affects inequality. James Galbraith addressed the difficulty of effectively measuring inequality, both at a national level and in attaining comparability across countries. He argued, contrary to Thomas Piketty's contention that capitalism inevitably leads to rising inequality, that the causes of inequality are, in fact, 'the artifact of particular moments in the history of financial capitalism, when strong pressures at the continental or global levels overwhelm the institutional defenses that societies seek to erect, whose purpose is to provide stabilising protections against the ravages of extreme inequality.'

Anthony Heath finished the day with a presentation on the unequal power relationships between groups, arguing that there is a mismatch between

> the standard political science approach to the study of power, which is much more concerned with the power which more or less organised groups possess, and the individualistic models of standard economic theory which typically ignore processes of social influence and organisation.

He noted that standard measures of inequality are all based on aggregated individual data, while, in fact, group-based differences in income or wealth are more likely to be drivers of adverse political outcomes such as political conflict, and suggested that we need a research agenda which understands the relationship between wealth inequality and political action.

References

Skidelsky, R. (2015). *The essential Keynes* (p. 262). London: Penguin.
Williams, B. (2004). *Truth and truthfulness*. Princeton, NJ: Princeton University Press.

Part I

Economics and Power: Basic Models of the Relationship

2

Power and Economics

Steven Lukes and Jonathan Hearn

Power and Economics by Steven Lukes

Power and economics are not often put together as a topic. Economists—although they regularly deploy notions such as market power and bargaining power—do so unreflectively: they have little, and usually nothing, to say about the concept of power, about what power is, and how to study it. It is, it would seem, either uninteresting or difficult for economists, and in particular mainstream economics, to deal with this notion. There is little about it in the literature of economics; if you look for articles and books about power in economics, you will find very few. There are

S. Lukes (✉)
New York University, New York, NY, USA

J. Hearn
University of Edinburgh, Edinburgh, UK

17

two interesting books, one by John Kenneth Galbraith[1] and another by Kenneth Boulding,[2] but they were maverick economists.

I was familiar with Galbraith's ideas while working on my own book on power, *Power: A Radical View*, which was published in 1974. Working further on a revised and expanded edition published in 2005, I turned to his book on power (published in 1983) and realized how relevant it was to what I was trying to argue, and I now see its continuing relevance to discussing the topic of this volume. Galbraith quotes another economist, Melville Ulmer, who contributed to one of the very few books on power and economics, actually entitled *Power and Economics*, a little Penguin book published 40 years ago.[3] Ulmer wrote, 'Perhaps no subject in the entire range of the social sciences is more important and at the same time so seriously neglected as the role of power in economic life.' And Galbraith himself says similar things in his book and offers, moreover, the beginnings of an explanation of why reflecting on power might be a problem for economists and, more widely, for anyone trying to understand the role of power in economic life. What Galbraith says, among other things, in *The Anatomy of Power* is:

> Nothing is so important in the defence of the modern corporation, as the argument that power does not exist; that all power is surrendered to the impersonal play of the market; all decision is in response to the instruction of the market. Nothing is more serviceable than the resulting conditioning of the young to that belief.[4]

What caught my interest in Galbraith's book is the idea of conditioning. Galbraith has three kinds of power. Indeed, it seems that everyone writing about power seems to want to have three kinds of it. (Why should power be triadic?) Galbraith's three kinds of power are: *condign* power (relying on threats or negative sanctions), *compensatory* power (relying on inducements), and *conditioned* power. He says of conditioned power:

---

[1] Galbraith (1983).
[2] Boulding (1990).
[3] Rothschild (1971).
[4] Galbraith (1983), p.120.

There is a successful expression of power when the individual submits to the purposes of others, not only willingly, but with a sense of attendant virtue. The supreme expression, of course, is when the person does not know that he or she is being controlled. This at the highest level is the achievement of conditioned power: belief makes submission not a conscious act, but a normal, natural manifestation of the approved behaviour.[5]

This thought was close to what I argued when I became involved in what came to be called 'the power debate' in the 1970s, which was generated within American political science but spread beyond it and is still alive. I welcome Jonathan Hearn's contribution to our discussion, since his recent book *Theorising Power*[6] admirably pulls together this debate alongside various other discussions of power, both in the Anglo-American and the European Continental traditions, and makes some pretty sharp criticisms of what I had to say.

I am also a triadic power theorist: my claim was that power should be viewed in three dimensions. C. Wright Mills, in the 1950s, wrote his great book *The Power Elite*, and his idea that there was a power elite (operating in three domains: the military, the governmental, and the corporate) in the USA was subjected to a healthy dose of scrutiny by Robert Dahl, the great American democratic theorist and political scientist. Dahl asked a very good question: What can be shown empirically about this claim that there is a cohesive elite in power? His answer was: We have to submit it to the empirical test of observability, we have to observe behaviour.

Dahl then came up, in his classic study of New Haven politics, *Who Governs?*, with the clear and straightforward idea that power consists in prevailing in decision-making where you can observe conflict over 'key issues' between actors in situations where there is a clear conflict of interests, those interests being revealed by preferences that are in conflict. The task was to trace the distribution of power, and thus determine whether there was unified power exhibited by some group that could be identified as a ruling elite. Dahl's conclusion was that what existed in New Haven was *pluralism*: there was no power elite in New Haven (and he would

[5] Galbraith (1983), p.160.
[6] Hearn (2012).

later maintain, across the nation), since different interests prevailed in decision-making over different issues.

This was *behaviourism*: the assumption that power is revealed by behaviour in decision-making situations. This approach was, in turn, criticised in a very influential article entitled 'Two Faces of Power' in the *American Political Science Review*. The political science profession widely discussed this article by Peter Bachrach and Morton Baratz, who claimed that power was not only revealed in decision-making, where you have observable conflict over issues in contention, but argued that there is also a second face, which is crucial to consider, that consists in what they (somewhat confusingly) called 'nondecision-making'. Who decides which issues reach the political arena? Who decides what is decided upon and how? This they called 'the mobilization of bias'—where some issues are organised into politics and others organised out. The whole issue of agenda control was thus raised by that very short and rather remarkable article, which they then elaborated in further articles and a book, *Power and Poverty*. Thus, a city or a country could be pluralistic in its decision-making but elitist in its nondecision-making.

I was impressed by this advance in thinking about power, but also dissatisfied. I decided to change the metaphor from *faces* of power to *dimensions*, because who could want two dimensions if you could have three? I was really trying to suggest that there is a way of looking beyond the two faces and seeing further and deeper into the phenomenon. So, I claimed that there is a third dimension of power, which has a clear relation to Galbraith's idea of conditioning, though it goes beyond it. For me the strategy of locating power by focusing on conflicting preferences, as revealed by observable behaviour, seemed inadequate; I was concerned with the question common among Marxist theorists, especially those influenced by Antonio Gramsci and the idea of hegemony, that there is something important to say about power over thought, desires, beliefs, and thus preferences.

I claimed in the little 1974 book that power can also be seen to be at work in shaping beliefs and preferences that can adversely affect people's interests. This should certainly be seen as itself an unduly narrow way of seeing the topic of power, because it focuses on power's *adverse* effects on people's interests and thus portrays power from a negative or pejorative perspective that assumes that people are better off when free from control by others. That limitation (which I later sought to correct) was path dependent: it resulted because of the way the debate until then was concerned with asymmetric, top-down power, or control, ways in which some are disadvantaged because others prevail. This perspective, as many went on to point out, neglected the many ways in which the power of some over others can be to the latter's advantage. My concern, however, was with (different) ways in which people's preferences can themselves be shaped by power.

This question bears directly on the relation between economics and the concept of power. How do interests relate to preferences? The question of how preferences are themselves shaped, rather than being assumed to be just exogenously given, seems to me an issue right at the centre of the discussion we need to have. Economists typically ignore or avoid it, or assume that the answer is straightforward. Hence the favoured expression 'revealed preferences'. Thus, for instance, George Stigler and Gary Becker write, 'It is neither necessary nor useful to attribute to advertising the function of changing tastes; advertising affects consumption not by changing tastes, but by changing price.'[7]

My claim, to repeat, was that power is not only to be seen in the first dimension, where you have observable conflict, where the most obvious case is visible and observable coercion—that is, cases where the question of who prevails is accessible to observation. It is not only, in the second phase, as claimed by Bachrach and Baratz, that power consists in suppressing or preventing from reaching the political arena grievances that are kept out of politics. It was always their unshakeable (still behaviourist) claim that these grievances—actual preferences of people whose access to the political decision-making process is blocked by observable mechanisms, either by neglect, but more often by deliberate agenda control, such as co-opting leaders—are, in turn, observable.

The grievances that are prevented from becoming effective political demands are themselves on this account observable. What interested me was the much more perplexing question of situations where people do not have grievances; where you can say that they have interests that do not become preferences, because of their beliefs: the shaping, in other

---

[7] Stigler and Becker (1977).

words, of beliefs that can be seen to be adversely affecting people's interests that are not revealed by their preferences.

As I proceeded with this it seemed to me there were further, more problematic questions that the idea of conditioned power, to use Galbraith's phrase, raises. Does power thus understood always have to involve *intention*? Is it possible that power can be exercised by affecting people's interests, thereby securing their compliance in ways that are not intended? Does the capacity that constitutes power—the power or capacity, in other words, to bring about compliance—always have to be intended? Bertrand Russell briskly defined power as 'the production of intended effects' and Max Weber, who wrote about power in a very pioneering and influential way, thought that power always had to be the expression of will. Is that so? I claimed, and still do, that power need not involve intention; that the most effective forms of power can be the result of others complying without the powerful even knowing it or intending it; for example, by merely following the dictates of roles and norms with unintended consequences. When managers in, say, corporations do their jobs and their companies accrue, or fail to accrue, profits, it need not be because the former intend the latter.

Does it necessarily even involve *action*? Why would we want to say that? Inaction can have significant consequences. Is it not the most effective form of power that others will comply with your interests without your having to lift a finger; without your having to *exercise* the power that you have, as when your status is enough to secure my compliance with your interests? As you can see, what I was up to was trying to expand and develop the concept of power, to broaden it in ways that end up by making it more and more problematic to study. Power has the remarkable feature of being at its most effective when it is least observable, by actors and by observers alike, which poses quite a neat paradox for the practice of social science.

It is rather obvious that this strategy of extending power's conceptual reach poses a range of problems, not only for social scientists, but also for anyone seeking evidence for significant, and in this case troubling, claims about how the world works. The kinds of claim I was making have been severely criticised and, over the years, I have tried to meet these criticisms. I conclude by all too briefly addressing three, the second and third of which have been most recently and most trenchantly formulated by Jonathan Hearn.

First, there is an objection which is quite widespread in the literature of the power debate. It registers an aversion to the very idea that people can have interests they do not perceive and acknowledge. The critique, in short, assumes (as economists generally do) that our interests are revealed by our preferences: that revealed preferences express people's interests. To think otherwise is to be presumptuous, even paternalistic. Who is the observer, let alone the social scientist, to attribute objective interests to subjects who do not recognise them? This is a tangled nest of issues, but here are three examples that should give such critics some trouble.

Consider, first, the repeal of the so-called death tax in the USA in 2001, and the fact that people widely believed that the death tax was against their interests. There is a fine book by Ian Shapiro and Michael Graetz[8] which documents the way in which this *framing* of what the estate tax meant had the effect of getting many people to believe that the so-called death tax was going to affect them and was a shocking thing. That is an example of one way in which people could be induced through the framing of an issue to believe something—in this case, that the estate tax was against their interests—which it was not.

In that case, there were anti-tax conservatives actively involved in propagating this highly effective framing of the issue in a way that favoured the interests of the rich and powerful. But such manipulative (i.e., active and intentional) exercising of power is not necessary. Consider the whole issue of the subordination of women, as exemplified in traditional societies, caste societies, or many other patriarchal societies, but also in the beauty myth and the gendered preoccupation with body size and weight in our own culture,[9] and in relationships where, despite sexual abuse and domestic violence, women can continue to view their abusers in a positive light. Are these not situations where three dimensional power is at work? A third example, which merits extensive discussion because of our very topic, is, indeed, hinted at by Galbraith himself in the citations above, in which he touches on how people can come to think about markets. Here, I can only point to what is called the 'performativity thesis'[10]; the idea

---

[8] Shapiro and Graetz (2006).
[9] See Bordo (2004).
[10] See MacKenzie, Muniesa, and Siu (2007).

that more and more of us are increasingly thinking, in more and more spheres of life, like economists, taking the social world to be as mainstream or neoclassical economic theories represent it, thereby rendering us blinder than before to the less observable operations of power.

That is all by way of saying that I claim that the idea that people may have preferences that are underpinned by beliefs that work against their interests is not an implausible idea. Adducing evidence and reasons to support such a claim is, of course, no simple matter, but when people say, 'How do you prove it?' I am inclined to reply, 'Are you really suggesting that this does not happen?' I believe that Jonathan and I are not in disagreement on this point.

The second criticism of my view (and the first of two that Jonathan offers) is to raise the real difficulty of determining just when explaining outcomes in terms of power is appropriate and when it is not. We need a way, as he points out, of identifying the powerful and the mechanisms at work that distinguish the operations of power from general socialisation and the internalisation of cultural norms. Also, we must recognise the obvious truth that there are countless impersonal social processes where concatenations of individuals' actions generate outcomes that may be intended by few or even no one, as when house buying choices by whites result in black ghettoes. (Hayek celebrates these, calling them 'catallaxies', with markets in mind, thus focusing exclusively on their mutually beneficial consequences).

To this, my response is to point to the link between locating power and attributing responsibility. In other words, when we want to find where power lies, our purpose is always to find out what is going on, discover the mechanisms, and identify actors, whether individual or collective, who could have acted otherwise, and who made a difference. Positing that they could have acted otherwise involves a counterfactual claim that there were other feasible possibilities, allied with the claim that there is a mechanism that could be identified as a casual process. There is a connection between power and responsibility that is inescapable. Cultures and impersonal social processes are enacted by human agents: cultural norms are promulgated, promoted, policed,[11] and enforced, and impersonal social processes can be encouraged and facilitated. Sometimes, cultural and structural explanations of troubling outcomes are proffered instead

---

[11] See Donzelot (1979).

of explanations in terms of politics and power, thereby deflecting out attention from the role of the powerful.

Finally, this last observation relates to the second criticism Jonathan makes: that, alongside writers like Pierre Bourdieu and Michel Foucault, I think of power in a critical way, so that, in my earlier work, I did assume it to take the form of *domination* and to be harmful to people's interests; that it is what he calls 'cryptic'; that there is something nefarious at work here; that, in short, studying and analysing power is a work of *debunking* and *unmasking*. As indicated above, I take this criticism seriously: power, viewed three dimensionally, can indeed be beneficial and empowering, and in diverse ways. This clearly suggests a direction in which the 'power debate' can be carried forward. Debunking illusions and unmasking hidden mechanisms cannot be all there is to critical social enquiry.

Power and Economics by Jonathan Hearn

Steven has invited me to put the emphasis on our disagreements. They are, of course, friendly disagreements, all within a shared tradition of thinking critically about society. I will try to respond to what Steven has said and do my best to relate it to the conference theme of power and economics. But, obviously, we are focused on the question of his third dimension of power, and disagreements about that. To some degree, we will need to leave the rest of the contributors to draw the wider connections.

Pretty clearly, the first and second dimensions of power are very relevant to economics. Many power struggles in the economic arena are quite manifest and observable contests, and many others happen behind the scenes, away from public view, but nonetheless ultimately observable. By somewhat crude analogy to formal politics, we might say some power struggles happen openly in the marketplace, and others 'around' the marketplace, in acts that constitute it in the first place. But we are preoccupied at the moment with the 'third dimension'. So, let me, following Steven, first try to restate what I understand to be the third dimension's defining features, then address whether power necessarily involves intention and action, and, finally, turn to the other areas of criticism Steven has raised, concluding with some remarks on the task of criticism.

The third dimension involves 'shaping beliefs and preferences that can adversely affect people's interests' according to Steven. Moreover, in its third dimension power operates by preventing grievances from arising, through 'shaped' preferences that fail to correspond to real interests. The main thing I would note here is that third dimensional power is fundamentally conceived as a critique of harm. While Steven allows that power need not be negative, and can even be beneficial, in the case of the third dimension, injury to people's true interests is the basic evidence that power is at work. This kind of power tends to correspond with what is commonly meant by 'domination'. However, it is worth noting that the defining feature of domination in this definition is found in the dominated, in their state of being harmed, of having a discrepancy between their interests and preferences; it is not found in the dominant, who are left relatively undefined.

Steven argues that power, especially in the third dimension, need not involve 'intention', or 'action'. The nub of the argument is that power is most effective when its operations are least observable. In other words, when all intention and action appears to come from those being dominated, acting on their apparent preferences. But this raises two puzzles. First, are the powerful in this case merely 'lucky', the dupes of good fortune? Or, is their capacity to be the passive recipients of the beneficial intentions and actions of others (less powerful), nonetheless due to actions and intentions that make this situation more likely? Actions and intentions are not discrete isolated events. Tending to treat them as such was one of the weaknesses of the behaviourist paradigm. Instead, they come in complex patterns. Steven's example of Shapiro and Graetz's study of the repeal of the California 'death tax' is a case in point. Voters voted their preference for repeal, against their own interests, and in the interests of the very wealthy. This was not simply a fortunate accident for the powerful. As he points out, they had a hand in orchestrating the voters' intentions and actions. Steven suggests that the subordination of women through such things as the 'beauty myth', or the naturalisation of the market in the popular imagination, provide even better examples of third dimensional power. However, the very fact that he raises these as problems, which we, his audience readily recognise, implies that they are not as ubiquitous and unquestioned as we might assume. Beliefs can be both prevalent and under question at the same time. Here, I would note that the recent focus on the performativity of markets in economic sociology is both an explanation of how markets become naturalised (in theorising markets as objects, economists help bring them into being), and a questioning of that naturalisation.

The second puzzle is this: if we define the third dimension of power in terms of harm done to interests, but we cannot connect this harm to intentions, it becomes very difficult to marshal a critique. Steven may intend a kind of 'consequentialism' here, where we are held responsible for the consequences of our actions, regardless of intent. But this certainly flies in the face of conventional moral and legal thought, in which responsibility is normally tied to intent. It would seem fruitless to try to build a position of critique disconnected from such conventions. There are of course in-between cases. In charges of 'manslaughter', we hold people responsible not for their intention to kill, but for their negligence in allowing death to happen. Thus, in the economic sphere we might want to distinguish the kind of harm done through deliberately mis-selling financial products or rigging LIBOR, from that done by failing to comprehend the implications of credit-default swaps and their liabilities. And, as Peter Morriss[12] has argued, we may want to allow a role for the critique of society, as a system with negative effects, which does not necessarily involve a critique of agents. It may be that highly liberalised forms of capitalism, in which capitals are insufficiently balanced by countervailing powers (to invoke J.K. Galbraith again), generate degrees of inequality that are systemically harmful to everyone's interests. Some might attribute the current Greek debt crisis to the irresponsible behaviour of Greek citizens and politicians, but others might see it as the outcome of an irrational European monetary and credit system as a whole.

Let me turn now to Steven's final three points. First, indeed, I agree with Steven that we must allow the possibility of claiming to understand people's interests better than themselves. As long as the capacity to make such claims is reciprocal, not the privilege of some group (academics? social scientists?), and claims are open to debate, I would see this premise as not just acceptable, but necessary for a free society. Respecting people's autonomy does not require placing their beliefs about their preferences

---

[12] Morriss (2002).

beyond dispute. Here, the distinction between 'interests' and 'preferences' is crucial, and a challenge to any economic theory that would not want to make this distinction. Clearly, Steven's conception of 'interests' is rooted in a notion of universal human goods (particularly autonomy and self-determination), while 'preferences' for him suggests a more contingent formation of wants and desires.

Second, yes; I think that we need to define the powerful in terms of their advantages, not just the subordinate in terms of the harm done to them. Without specifying the powerful, it is difficult to distinguish the 'shaping of preferences' from basic socialisation. Simply being a member of society is itself in some sense limiting—we are bound by shared norms. But we do not want to treat all instances of this kind of constraint as 'harm', as being subject to power. Steven's response is that we must connect power and responsibility. But how do we do this if we have demoted 'intention and action' in our definition of power? Yes, we can posit counterfactual scenarios in which the powerful could have acted otherwise. But if this is to be more than the banal observation that life and history can take many different paths, the 'could have' needs to become a 'should have', which implies some intent and foresight[13] on the part of the actor.

Finally, I have indeed argued that Steven's concept of the third dimension is akin to others like Bourdieu's 'habitus' and Foucault's notion of 'subjectivity' as a construct of power relations. All of these place special emphasis on the hidden operations of power, what I have called 'cryptic domination'.[14] But the problem here is not one of being critical per se. I think there is a proper role for social critique, and for the critique of power. My point is that it is often suggested that these forms of cryptic domination take us to the heart of what must be critiqued, and I disagree. My point is that there are plenty of more readily discernible operations of power that can be more fruitfully critiqued, whose legitimacy can be more effectively challenged. If we become preoccupied with the question, 'Why do people not see that they are being dominated?', we focus our attention on the sad state of the dominated, to the neglect of the dominant, and how domination is done. I think more can be achieved through

---

[13] See Wrong (2002).
[14] Hearn (2012).

the more mundane task of clearly ascribing power to certain actors, defining what might make that power legitimate, and questioning whether it is legitimate. I worry about inviting too many bright young minds to puzzle over the mysteries of invisible power, to the neglect of more discernible and tractable problems of power. The critique of power must work in the light, or at least the half-light, of claims and counter-claims about legitimacy. To define power as hidden in its very nature is actually to put it beyond critique. Even Galbraith's idea of 'conditioned power' suggests that while it is usually taken for granted, as in Steven's opening quote from Galbraith about the unquestioned power of the market, the social mechanisms that produce and reproduce it—schooling, media, advertising, moral authorities, and so on—are normally well-known, and susceptible to scrutiny. Critique as such begins not with the question 'Why don't we see it?', but with 'Why do we, and why should we, accept it?'

References

Bordo, S. (2004). *Unbearable weight: Feminism, western culture, and the body* (2nd ed., 10th anniversary ed.). Oakland, CA: University of California Press.

Boulding, K. E. (1990). *Three faces of power*. Thousand Oaks, CA: Sage.

Donzelot, J. (1979). *Policing families*. New York: Pantheon.

Galbraith, J. K. (1983). *The anatomy of power*. New York: Houghton Mifflin.

Hearn, J. (2012). *Theorizing power*. Basingstoke/New York: Palgrave Macmillan.

MacKenzie, D., Muniesa, F., & Siu, L. (Eds.). (2007). *Do economists make markets: On the performativity of economics*. Princeton: Princeton University Press.

Morriss, P. (2002). *Power: A philosophical analysis* (2nd ed., pp. 40–42). Manchester: Manchester University Press.

Rothschild, K. W. (Ed.). (1971). *Power in Economics: Selected readings*. Harmondsworth: Penguin.

Shapiro, I., & Graetz, M. *Death by a thousand cuts: The fight over taxing inherited wealth* (New ed.). Princeton: Princeton University Press.

Stigler, G. J., & Becker, G. S. (1977, March). *The American Economic Review, 67*(2), 84.

Wrong, D. (2002). *Power: Its forms, bases and uses* (3rd ed., p. 2). London: Transaction.

3

Economics as Superstructure

Norbert Häring and Lucas Zeise

Economics as Superstructure by Norbert Häring

What I am going to talk about follows on directly from what we have just discussed, the power of shaping beliefs and preferences, and the role of economics in that exercise. To pay tribute to the Marxist title that Robert has suggested for my talk 'Economics as Superstructure', I would like to start with a (slightly abbreviated) quote from Karl Marx: 'The ideas of the ruling class are in every epoch the ruling ideas. The ruling ideas are nothing more than the ideal expression of the dominant material relationships; the relationships that make the one class the ruling one; therefore the ideas of its dominance.'

I am not a Marxist, and I have always had trouble with the Marxist jargon, which is why I brought Lucas Zeise to explain it to me and to all of you. In my own words, the quote says that not all economic ideas are

N. Häring (✉)
Handelsblatt, Dusseldorf, Germany

L. Zeise
Financial Times Deutschland, Hamburg, Germany

created equal. Some ideas make it into the leading economic journals and others can hardly be published. Some ideas make those who develop them successful in academia or even famous and very influential, other ideas sentence those who dare develop them to a life at the margin at best. Ideally, you would think this would be a function of how convincing the idea is, and how good the academic is at developing it, writing it down and marketing it, but we all know that excellence by itself does not get you very far in this business.

Another very important ingredient for a successful career in economics is how convenient your subject of study and your results are to the powerful in society. This is what Marx says: economics, like all social sciences, is a product of the prevailing economic and political conditions, and it has a role to fulfil in these conditions. If the interests of the powerful change, which is a corollary of that, so will economics, and that is how I am going to structure my piece here. I will give you some examples of how economics changed through the decades and centuries, and how that conformed to changing interests of the powerful.

My first example is the switch from mercantilism to the free trade doctrine of David Hume, Adam Smith and David Ricardo in the eighteenth century. Before the British discovered free trade, the nation had been following a protectionist industrialisation policy. Starting with Henry VII in 1485, the strategy turned Britain from a poor exporter of raw materials to a leading exporter of cloth. Henry levied export taxes on wool and gave privileges to wool manufacturers. As the British capacity to manufacture wool increased, he, and later his successors, raised these export duties on wool. Finally, Elizabeth I banned wool exports altogether, so that only manufactured cloth could be exported. This is how Britain became the leading producer and exporter of manufactured goods. *Only* after it had succeeded in that, and this predominance was firmly established, did British economists start to preach free trade to the world.

Coming back to Jonathan's argument about harm, I would say this was very patriotic of Adam Smith and David Hume, and something that really furthered British interests and did no harm. But the question is: What about the others? Who are we talking about if we ask if there is harm? Many fell for it in other countries; Britain was also very dominant in exporting ideas. But not everybody believed in the new gospel. There were the ones like Friedrich List in Germany, or Alexander Hamilton in the USA, who took it as what it was: the attempt of the British to pull up the ladder that they had climbed up to industrial dominance; and the same would happen again in the USA.

Starting with Alexander Hamilton, the country pursued a protectionist trade and industrialisation strategy, and it also was very successful at it. Only after the USA had become an industrial leader did its economists start to preach the gospel of unconditional free trade; it is no coincidence that this turn in the convictions of economists happened in America considerably later than in Britain. The country, and thus also the powerful in this country, had developed an interest in promoting free trade much later than Britain.

As a second example I would like to point you to the emergence of the neoclassical doctrine around the middle to the late nineteenth century. This was the time that Karl Marx told workers that they were being exploited and the threat of revolution was rife everywhere. The dominant doctrine was classical economics at the time, and classical economics was not a good antidote to Marxism. Adam Smith would not have disagreed too much with Marx on exploitation, as you can tell from the following, slightly abbreviated quote from Smith:

> What are the common wages of labour, depends everywhere upon the contract usually made between those two parties, whose interests are by no means the same. [...] It is not [...] difficult to foresee which of the two parties must, upon all ordinary occasions, have the advantage in the dispute, and force the other into a compliance with their terms. [...] The masters can hold out much longer. [...] Though they did not employ a single workman, [they] could generally live a year or two upon the stocks which they have already acquired. Many workmen could not subsist a week.

Smith clearly saw very unequal power there, and he had the wages determined by this unequal power relationship, and not by some market forces. That was not convenient, so it had to go. It was not an admissible attitude for economists any more, once workmen were threatening to use force to end exploitation. Economists who wanted to preserve capitalism needed to overcome the classical economists' analysis of wages as a product of negotiation power. The following is how neoclassical pioneer

John Bates Clark formulated the challenge: 'Workmen, it is said, are regularly robbed of what they produce; this is done by the natural working of competition. If this charge were proved, every right-minded man should become a socialist.'[1]

That was his introduction to his famous book, and clearly his answer would be, 'No, it cannot be proved, we do not have to become socialists'. He and some others developed marginal productivity theory and that theory rose to the challenge of disproving the charge of exploitation. His theory claimed that at the margin every factor of production, including labour, was remunerated exactly with what it contributed to the final product. Thus, power was out of the game; of course, workmen and communists still discussed it, but you did not have to answer them directly, you could say, 'Well, everybody gets what they deserve, it is okay.'

It is interesting to note another aspect of the early neoclassical theory; the early neoclassicals were quite open to redistribution. They still saw marginal utility decline with income so they considered redistribution from rich to poor a welfare-increasing policy. At that particular time, that was not against the interest of enlightened rulers. You have to remember, this was the time when Bismarck introduced social security in Germany explicitly with the goal of appeasing workers and helping to fend off the threat of revolution. The rich needed to be convinced, with the help of a convenient economic theory, that some limited redistribution of income was to their own advantage, as it helped to preserve the status quo that was favourable to them.

That takes us to the third change of doctrine, which I would like to highlight. By the 1930s, the main threat for the wealthy had shifted from revolution to redistribution enforced by a democratic majority. It was also a time of preparation for war. Thus, the priorities of the rich and the rulers had shifted to discrediting redistribution and towards making the best use of national resources. And economics abided again. As a first step, Lionel Robbins and others banned interpersonal utility comparison, which were so favourable to the idea of redistribution. Robbins redefined economics to be the science that studies human behaviour as a relationship between ends and scarce means, which has alternative uses. This

---

[1] Clark (1899).

convenient dogmatic change had the effect of pushing distributional concerns outside economics; economic efficiency became the sole target, and as redistribution often comes in the way of efficiency it could be argued that redistribution was bad. Economic reason came to be associated with as little redistribution as possible.

The fourth example of a shift in economic doctrine suiting the interests of the powerful is a continuation of the third. It is the emergence and eventual predominance of methodological individualism and of the anti-collectivist schools of thought, called rational choice and public choice.

It was the time of the cold war; economists were enlisted in the ideological battle to win the minds and hearts of the people for capitalism. The aim was to focus attention on the strong point of capitalism—efficiency of allocation—and to discredit what socialism claimed as its strong points—planning, collaboration, and fairness of distribution.

Ken Arrow ostensibly proved that it was impossible to come to rational collective decisions. Anthony Downs, Mancur Olson, and James Buchanan built on this and portrayed the government and trade unions as the enemies of liberty. The more government did, the bigger was the threat to liberty.

At the other extreme are those ideas which the powerful do not like to be discussed at all.

These were the four examples, all taken from my book *Economists and the Powerful*,[2] of how economics shifted the interests of the powerful. I would like to spend a few more minutes talking about what is not to be talked about in economics. The first thing that comes to mind is power itself; market power is there, but power by itself is hardly ever there. The powerful have a need to legitimise their power. If that is not viable, they like their power to be downplayed as much as possible to the point of becoming invisible; that is, what we have discussed as the third dimension. This is what mainstream economics is doing: if you look at the index of a random economics textbook the chances are very good that you will not find the entry 'power' in the index.

Power is tantamount to the absence of competition and the opposite is also true; perfect competition, the darling of mainstream economics, is

---

[2] Häring (2012).

tantamount to the absence of power. This is why treating the economy as if something close to perfect competition was the rule has a very important political implication; it negates the presence and importance of power. While it is true that there are all these rich theories around that do have a part for power, if you look at what is in the public debate and what economists say about taxes and social security contributions, it is all based on the naïve textbook perfect competition. Labour market institutions and taxes are always bad and harmful. All these more advanced models that say otherwise are good to have, to be able to say that economics is not as one-sided and simple-minded as critics claim. But they do not influence to a significant extent the input of the profession to public debate.

That is particularly important in the labour market: if you pretend that workers routinely have a next best alternative to their current job, which is only marginally less attractive, there is no power of the employer, there is no justification for unions, for lay-off protection and for employment benefits. In particular, if you are in Germany, that is exactly where economists who are in any way influential start from, that is what they equate with economic reason; everything else is some sort of aberration that you have to convince people you really need less of. If you pretend that market power is the exception and not the rule, you cannot tax companies without doing a great deal of harm. You cannot ask for higher wages without causing unemployment. If you pretend that there is a well-functioning market for top managers, CEOs will have no real power, and you will need to reward them very handsomely for any value that they help to create. Such assumptions, which define power away, almost always yield results that are very much in the interests of the powerful.

The second example of something that is not to be talked about is money: 'money is power' goes the saying, so that already connects it. If it is power it cannot be talked about, and that is why the powerful do not like it to be discussed and mainstream economics is, again, abiding. Banks putting out targets of 25% and achieving them were not considered excessively powerful by economists; they were declared efficient and successful, and something to strive for. Financial institutions that individually control the flow of billions of dollars do not have any power that is worth analysing for mainstream economists. Even in the leading macroeconomic models, including those used by central banks like the

Federal Reserve or the European Central Bank, there is no money to speak of in those models; they have a model that does not include what they are doing—quite bizarre, but it serves its purpose.

These are examples of how the ideas suit those who are in power, and I find this a very productive way of thinking. In contemporary discussions about economics, the trap is to think about who is right and who is wrong; I think about who does this idea serve and who does that idea serve, and that is usually much more revealing and rewarding. It has its limits, and it is usually at the limits that it becomes most interesting when you start to think: 'Do they really know what their interest is?' For example, in Germany, there often is a very one-sided discussion among the German economists and politicians that is very different from everybody around them, including the Anglo-Saxons or the South Europeans. In these cases, one has to wonder: 'Do they understand that even as a creditor, you have to become lenient at some point or you are harming your own interests?' 'Have they just fallen into the trap of believing their own propaganda and do they not know any more what is good for them, or is there a deeper idea behind why they still do and believe what they do?'

You can think about all sorts of complications: it might be a nice idea, on some level, that Germany should be interested in the prosperity of southern Europe, so that it can sustainably export to these countries. But when we are living in a resource-constrained world, you could include the fact that there are just not enough resources for everybody to be prosperous. Maybe at some deeper level it is not a bad idea to shake off some of those countries and let them become poorer and less resource-intensive. Maybe the goal is to move to some sort of neo-colonial core-centre-relationship, where Germany and France form the industrial core and the South provides tourism, raw materials and agricultural goods. Who knows: these are the interesting fringes of this way of thinking.

Economics as Superstructure by Lucas Zeise

I perfectly agree with what Norbert has said, so I will add very few remarks to it. To my mind, we have heard some excellent examples for how economic theories have adapted to certain needs. Why do economists at certain junctures in time develop certain ideas? Ideas spring up and are developed to fulfil certain functions that become useful for the ruling class of a nation or a group of nations. They are, as your Marx quotation says, the ideas of the ruling class; consequently, the prevalent and hence ruling ideas in the whole of society: that is, what we call the mainstream.

The first remark I want to make concerns the title of your speech 'Economics as Superstructure'. Superstructure, in German *Überbau*, is Marxist terminology, and it refers to the whole of social institutions. It refers to the state, the law, and it refers to the ideology; that is, religion and science. In Marx's thinking, this superstructure develops on what is called the 'basis', which is what we call the 'economy'. The economy is the 'basis of society' on which the other social relations, the state, the law, science, religion, and the arts are built.

On the other hand, the superstructure is necessary to establish and keep up the economic conditions of production, which is a roundabout way of saying the economy. To establish markets, to provide workers and labour markets, you need governments, laws, education systems, and all of that. The class system of society is established and stabilised by a super-structure that, on the one hand, is built upon the economy, and, on the other, keeps the economy in its class structure, in its capitalist mode. Science and, of course, economics are part of that superstructure.

One consequence of this is that, for understanding society and the history of mankind, you have to look at the economic conditions; you have to do economics. As all the other social relations—that is, the superstructure—are developed in such a way as to keep the economy going, they can only be understood if you understand what the continuation of the economic structure requires. It follows that economics is the basic science for all other social sciences. And after the young philosopher Karl Marx had discovered this simple truth, he turned to economics and started studying Smith, Ricardo and the wonders of the English capitalist economy.

There is another pertinent consequence of this philosophical position. And that is, what Norbert has concentrated on: economics is a science that is not exclusively, but primarily developed to keep down the lower classes. This is the gist of what Norbert said. It presupposes that we do have a class structure. And as the topic of the conference that lead to this volume was power, we should talk about class structure. Power and class structure begin with the division of labour very early in human history. As economists and/or as sociologists, we are not interested in what power constitutes in principle as a relationship between individuals but as that which constitutes society: the relationship between classes. This relationship is power. You cannot begin to understand an economic system if you do not concentrate on the power relations between the classes and, of course, between the individuals as members of these classes. You do not understand how the feudal economy and society works if you do not understand that the lord tells the peasant what to grow and lives off his produce. You cannot hope to understand the capitalist economy and society if you neglect the basic fact that the capitalist tells the workers on what to work and derives his profits from their labour.

Economics is not the only science that is used or abused in the way Norbert described it; namely, to justify the power relations that be. All social science is used or abused in this way to produce 'false consciousness'. Among the sciences, economics is particularly prone to this abuse, probably because this political science has achieved a special status among the social sciences: a status of perceived objectivity. It is close to the way applied natural sciences like medicine or engineering are socially recognised; that is why economics as a science is so particularly useful for the ruling class.

This, of course, is in stark contrast to the common way of looking at it; economics is meant in that common way to further the understanding of the way societies work, to make us understand the various ways how people secure their livelihood, and to help us find ways to promote their and our welfare. Classical and neoclassical economics both reconcile these two uses of economics by stating plainly that the established order is all for the common good. A modern version of this is the trickle-down theory. The real classical version is the fable the patrician Menenius Agrippa tells rebellious plebeians in Shakespeare's *Coriolanus*. You probably know the fable; it is the fable of the stomach and the body members. It goes like this: it is all for the good that the stomach gets all the food first, and divides it after that between the members of the body. Their protest against the stomach's privilege turns out to be silly, as they are all part of the same body and they are in the same boat and have to work together. I have looked up Wikipedia on this, and that tells me

that the story is even older than the Latin authors Plutarch and Livy—
Shakespeare's sources. It can be traced to ancient Egypt, and that sounds
really plausible when we look at the pyramids; you really needed good
stories to convince the people of Egypt to work those many, many stones
and put the pyramids together.

One should think that, on the other hand, the ruling class and their
political agents require some sort of economics that produces real insight
into the way society works; and sometimes it does that. The question is
always how much insight is being produced, and how much this insight
is counteracted by the fact that you have to produce ideology to justify
the given state of affairs. Pure ideology—pure justification of the existing
order—will not deliver good, truthful results. Yet, I suspect that nobody
really minds. Decisions on economic policy have hardly ever been based
on sound and unprejudiced economic theory.

Let us consider one interesting example. In 2008, Lehman Brothers
fell down and the whole financial system was in disarray. Shortly afterwards, the Queen went to a reception at the London School of Economics
department. She asked, 'Why didn't you foresee this mess?' I think the
economists present knew why this mess was not foreseen. To my mind,
it is quite obvious. It is because it disturbs the business, not of the economists themselves, but of their employers. It is harmful sometimes to
mention a development that is not good for your business. Even if you
calculate that a crash or a financial crisis is coming or even inevitable, it
is better not to mention it.

In Norbert's examples about the rise and fall of economic theories,
there happen to be economists who found pleasant or suitable answers
to awkward questions. We can assume that it is not sheer chance that a
researcher or author economist stands at the ready to adapt the relevant
theory in a way suitable to the powers that be. The mainstream does
not happen by chance, probability or the sheer number of economists
swimming in it. It is produced or, more precisely, it is managed. Much
effort and money are spent on raising the politically correct theories and
promoting the theorists. Thus, we are, nowadays, asked to look with awe
at the history of the Mont Pelerin Society as a successful example for
managing the mainstream. What a long-term project that was and, more

astonishingly, after this resounding victory they have achieved, they are still at it and hungry.

Great success stories, in that sense, can also be found in the somewhat less spectacular day-to-day business of managing the mainstream. For example, German universities and research institutes are almost devoid of any trace of Keynesianism and are totally clean of even faintly Marxist-type economists. Even more obvious is the fact that banks and other private institutions have to select their economists with care. A few stars in this business are quite successful at being unorthodox but, even then, there are limits. The largest German bank, for example, can evidently not tolerate a chief economist who tells you a few pertinent things about the way the money system works.

References

Clark, J. B. (1899). *The distribution of wealth: A theory of wages, interest and profits* (p. 4). New York: Macmillan.
Häring, N. (2012). *Economists and the powerful*. London: Anthem Press.

4

Economics as Science

Nancy Cartwright and John Bryan Davis

Economics as Science by Nancy Cartwright

The plan for this talk is to discuss, first, the question 'What is science?' I'm going to explain that the second question, 'Does economics fit the bill?', is hard to answer since we have no good answer to the first question. Then I shall turn to the question, 'Does economics' standing as a science give it special power?' Here, I shall point out that whether its knowledge constitutes science or not, economics does have esoteric knowledge that provides it with hidden sources of power.

My predecessor by several years at the London School of Economics, Karl Popper, thought he had the question 'What's a science?' solved. As you all know, scientific claims, he maintained, are falsifiable: 'I found that those of my friends who were admirers of Marx, Freud and Adler were impressed by [...] their apparent explanatory power. These theories appeared able to

N. Cartwright (✉)
University of Durham, Durham, UK

J.B. Davis
Marquette University, Milwaukee, USA

© The Editor(s) (if applicable) and The Author(s) 2016
R. Skidelsky, N. Craig (eds.), *Who Runs the Economy?*,
DOI 10.1057/978-1-137-58017-7_4

explain practically everything that happened within the fields to which they referred […] It was precisely this fact—that they always fitted, that they were always confirmed—which in the eyes of their admirers constituted the strongest argument in favor of those theories. It began to dawn on me that this apparent strength was in fact their weakness.'[1]

Here is an example that would have been dear to Popper's heart, just the kind he gives himself. The Rat Man, according to Freud, had an unconscious desire to hurt his father. This could, of course, result in him being nasty to his father. But it could also quite unexpectedly result in his being nice to his father through various Freudian mechanisms we all know about. So, the hypothesis is consistent with incompatible bits of data.

The first trouble, if we adopt Popper's criterion, is that it lets in too much. The claim that I am not sitting at my desk in Durham or in UCSD at this very moment is falsifiable, but it is certainly not science. You would need to add a whole lot more restriction to zero in on science and it is then the 'whole lot more' that does the bulk of the job. Worse, we have had considerable trouble figuring what the whole lot more is.

The second trouble is that it rules out too much. Physics has exactly the same problem as Freudian theory. The very same hypothesis about a situation can imply very different observations. Consider, for example, 'This ionised thallium has undergone beta decay' as the hypothesis. This implies two observations that are incompatible with each other: (1) that the ionised thallium has been replaced by fully ionised lead, with a continuum-state electron and anti-neutrino emitted; and (2) that it has been replaced by hydrogen-like lead with an anti-neutrino emitted. The physics solution to this is the obvious one we all know, that which observations are implied depends on what other empirical facts are taken to obtain in the situation. But that was exactly Freud's solution too! (Of course, one can then begin to puzzle out whether you then put some constraints on these other auxiliary assumptions. That attempt, too, has met with little success.)

The long and short of it is that we have not made much headway in saying what is science after 60 years of serious work in the philosophy of science. And not only in the philosophy of science but elsewhere: people are very concerned about climate change deniers, whether, when they

---

[1] Popper's 'Conjectures and Refutations', originally published 1963 (2013).

produce arguments, the arguments are really proper science; people in the USA are concerned about whether you can teach creationism in the public schools as a science along with evolution; the US Supreme Court's *Daubert* ruling worries about what can count as scientific expertise; and so on. None of these have come up with any satisfactory criterion to demarcate science from non-science. This past autumn, the Philosophy of Science Association, at their big international biannual meeting, after many, many years of the issue lying dormant, had a session on 'What is the scientific method?' Nothing came of it.

So, it is a little hard to answer the question 'Is economics a science?' My answer is that I do not have a clue.

I take it I am supposed to address whether an economist has particular power as a scientist rather than, for instance, as an adviser to public policy, running the Bank of England and so on. The first thing to note is that the power stemming from economics as science surely depends not entirely on the truth of the claim that it is a science, but on the perception—and there is a wide perception—that economics is a science and, as was mentioned earlier, a particularly good science because it is (at least, is thought to be) objective. It cannot be denied that (by contrast with sociology or anthropology, for instance) economics gets special kudos in policy areas and with the public because it is thought to be, it purports to be, it is widely believed to be objective and part of the reason for that is that it is quantitative. Quantitative is thought to be particularly objective. I will not go into this much—you are probably familiar with Ted Porter's *Trust in Numbers* and Michael Power's *The Audit Society*, both of which describe both the history and some sociology of how we have been converted to the idea that if something is quantitative it is objective, and if it is not quantitative it is most in danger of not being objective.

I would like to go on to talk a little about hidden sources of power. Economics as a science, because it produces knowledge and knowledge claims, has sources of power that many of you might recognise but certainly are not publicly recognised. The two I want to talk about are looping effects and then the hidden power that comes through the design of measures and models.

Looping effects have a number of other names: performativity, reflexivity—the word that George Soros likes so much—self-fulfilling prophesies.

I will just give you as an example one case—the Black-Sholes model—that you are surely familiar with, studied by Donald MacKenzie, the sociologist at Edinburgh. Here is how MacKenzie and Millo describe it: 'Option pricing theory [...] succeeded empirically not because it discovered pre-existing price patterns but because markets changed in ways that made its assumptions more accurate and because the theory was used in arbitrage [...] Option pricing theory [...] did not simply describe a pre-existing world, but helped create a world of which the theory was a truer reflection.'[2] So, MacKenzie and Millo conclude, 'In so doing they altered patterns of pricing in a way that increased the validity of the model's predictions.'

So, that is one source of power, where you have these looping effects.[3] This is a very explicit case where there is a clear causal chain that MacKenzie traces. The other, of course, is Michel Foucault's theme that anyone who is able to create a new category or new concept that comes to be prominent can have a hidden source of power: as the concept becomes dominant, people begin to use it. They identify themselves to be in the category and begin to act accordingly and they identify others as in the category and treat them in the ways deemed appropriate. Like 'the involuntarily unemployed', the old example of the 'deserving poor' and so forth. That is one source of power that is not always so obvious to people outside economics.

Another hidden source of power over people's lives that economics has is in *the design of measures and of models*. I am going to talk about measures first, illustrating with cases from Tony (A.B.) Atkinson. These are places where having economic knowledge really matters; you would not know what you were doing if you did not have this economic knowledge. I teach this material when we talk about whether or not economics is objective in the sense of being value-free. These are all places where making certain decisions, based reliably on knowledge that you have as an economist and reasonably reliable predictions about how the measures will be used, will fairly predictably harm some groups of people and benefit others. There is often no scientific reason to make the decision one way rather than another. So you can, consciously or not, use your

---

[2] MacKenzie and Millo (2003).

[3] But as Michel Foucault argues, this source of power is not confined to economics but works for any science whose concepts get a grip on the way members of society and its institutions see themselves and others.

economic knowledge to benefit one group or another. This is an easy place for the intrusion of values—and it tends to be hidden. It depends on special economic knowledge that most people do not have and thus cannot see what difference it makes whether the measure is designed one way or another. Yet, given groups will be benefited and harmed, given the natural uses that we know will be made of the measures.

Here is just one issue Atkinson raises when you are thinking about designing a poverty measure. People can get the idea of the difference between an absolute and a relative measure; you can sometimes even get people to think, if it is a relative measure, about what they would like the poverty line to be relative to, like two-thirds of the median income. But if you start asking about whether it should be the mean, the median or the mode, you have lost most people. In Atkinson's book on poverty measures,[4] you find in chapter after chapter places where it makes a big difference to the poverty numbers and poverty ranking of different states and nations depending on how you design the measure in the detail—whether you choose relative versus absolute, mean versus median, whether you measure expenditure versus income, whether you treat households versus families, whether you use equivalent scales, numbers versus gaps. For many purposes, Atkinson favours measuring a poverty gap, which is how deeply below the poverty line individuals are as opposed to just counting the numbers. If we just count the numbers to measure poverty, then if you want to be seen to reduce poverty, it is a good strategy to take the people at the top and push them over.

Here is one really easy example of how important the details can be. The Indian Statistical Institute used to ask people how much rice they had consumed over the previous 30 days as part of their poverty measure. In response to criticisms that 30 days is too long a period and people do not remember how much rice they have consumed over the last 30 days, India changed their time period to seven days, a period that many other countries use. The technical change cut the Indian national poverty rate by half. By redesigning the measure, 175 million Indians suddenly escaped poverty.[5] Those are the kind of issues that come up in the

[4] Atkinson, 1998, Poverty in Europe, Wiley-Blackwell http://eu.wiley.com/WileyCDA/WileyTitle/productCd-0631209093.html
[5] Deaton (2001) p. 139.

design of measures. Atkinson also raises a variety of similar issues about the design of EU measures for social exclusion.

Let us look next at the hidden power that economics has in its ability to settle on *modelling assumptions*, both in the choice of model type and also in the choice of details within the model. First, consider the choice of the model type. Here is another case I take from Atkinson. He draws our attention to the fact that the commonly used representative agent models conceal issues of distribution. This is somewhat like Norbert Häring's point, where he argued that economic theory changed as the interests of the well-off changed. How it changed, in almost all of his cases, was by burying issues. Certain issues were no longer salient. They were not expressible in the model so they became hidden. It is not that you cannot talk about them, but you cannot talk about them when you are doing 'proper' economics within the model. Or consider this: most models assume the aim is to maximise expected utility. Of course, you can make utility the most abstract notion possible, but still there is a difference between looking for a course of action that maximises expected utility and one that maximises something like the substantial freedom of Amartya Sen's capability approach to just distribution.

On assumptions within a model, choice of parameters is a famous case. Nicholas Stern got in a great deal of trouble about the choice of parameters in the *Stern Review of the Economics of Climate Change*. The *Review* begins with a maximise-expected-utilities model. Interestingly, it is a representative agent model: there is one representative from each generation and Stern admits that the *Review* thus does not really take on issues about the distribution of responsibilities and benefits within any generation, so he does not really talk about who pays; for example, rich countries or poor countries. That is concealed in the representative agent model, but Stern is upfront that he is doing that.

The question that raised controversy is how much weight we should assign to each generation. If you look at the sum of expected utilities in such a model, you have to include a weight for each representative agent. Economists are all used to putting discount factors for the future into equations, but you have to think about what this discount factor for the future means in this equation. There is a variety of reasons for discounting the future. For instance, future generations might not be there, so you might want to count future generations a little less. Or, it could be a very poor way of putting uncertainty into the model, since this is not where a hedge against the uncertainly of our predictions belongs. When you put a weight in the *Stern Review* model you are weighting how much utility that generation matters in the proposed policy. The discount factors really matter here and what is interesting to me is that, once you have chosen an expected-utilities framework, you cannot avoid this question. You can fail to write a weight down there but that then that means you are weighting everybody equally, or you can discount some generations relative to others, but you cannot avoid the issue. Simply by virtue of using the expected-utilities framework in this case, you are forcing some ethical decisions to be made.

The reason I bring this up in this context is not really to point out the ethics of it so much as to point out that, if you look at the *Stern Review*, you have to be fairly sophisticated to see what is going on there. It takes a good understanding of what the modelling means to see that using an expected-utilities framework unavoidably raises this issue about how future generations are treated, and to understand and evaluate the different claims in the debate about the exact form of the discount factors.

Just to review: the promulgation of economic claims, I have reminded you, can change the world. Economics can even do this by making the world adjust to fit its otherwise probably false models. Moreover, details matter in measures and models. They affect policy and who benefits and who loses. The point is that it takes real economic knowledge to understand how these effects occur in both those kinds of cases. So, does economics have power because it is a science, because of those special kinds of knowledge that economics has? The answer is *yes*.

Economics as Science by John Bryan Davis

I will begin by identifying myself a little. I was trained originally in analytic philosophy, not at Oxford but in the Oxford style. Then, I was trained in economics, primarily history of economics. I am co-editor of the *Journal of Economic Methodology*, and I chaired and taught in a History and Philosophy of Economics programme for 10 years at the University of

Amsterdam, where the programme focus was the History of Economics from 1980 to the Present. I was, and am still, especially interested in the evolution of mainstream economics. A principal argument that I have made is that all the main new movements in mainstream economics are sourced from outside economics—behavioural economics, for example, from psychology. I was interested in what this meant for the state of economics. Sometimes, I am charged with arguing economics exhibits 'mainstream pluralism'. I will talk here about mainstream economics at this stage of its development as essentially a performative science. I want to emphasise the relation of economics to inequality and social stratification.

I think it is fair to say that we live in a world that is becoming increasingly unequal. It is also being institutionalised as such, and this works through structures that enhance and reinforce social stratification. I have worked with recent economics stratification theory as a foundation for self-reinforcing inequality and stratification processes that result from structures that systematically privilege higher and de-privilege lower socio-economic strata. Where is the science of economics in all this? The economics profession's own stratification processes involve replacement of its traditional independent reflexive practices for the evaluation and assessment of economics research with a stratification-reinforcing journal-ranking system that perpetuates status quo economics, limits innovation in economics, and thus serves social stratification.

The effect of this process in economics, I suggest, is that scientific behaviour in mainstream economics is increasingly replaced by bureaucratic behaviour and economics increasingly functions as what I will describe as a performative science in the sense of a science that always sees the world in its own image. I suggest that mainstream economics then risks becoming a 'bubble-science', one that is vulnerable to collapse like alchemy and other failed sciences of the past, and, as such, a potential contributor to economic crises. Let me explain this in terms of the change in reflexive practice in economics.

What was previously the traditional form of reflexive practice in economics? In the past, *economic methodology* and the *history and philosophy of economics* were economics' reflexive domains; in effect, its principal forms of scientific self-consciousness. Like other sciences, economics relies on a theory-evidence relationship. *Economic methodology* explains the theory-evidence relationship as a reflexive relationship. Theory depends on evidence and what counts as evidence is influenced by theory. Yet, because the economy itself evolves, there must always be new evidence so, for economic methodology, theory is always evolving and there must always be new theory. The *history and philosophy of economics* then explains economics' status as a science relative to the adequacy of its methodological practice and, in particular, according to its ability to evolve as a science.

What is economics' new reflexive practice? Methodology and the history and philosophy of economics are now largely marginalised in the economics profession. Whereas those reflexive domains were the means by which research quality and economics' performance as a science was ultimately judged, research quality is now judged largely through journal-ranking systems. Comments have been made in the discussion here about the importance of institutions and apparatuses like the Research Assessment Exercise in the UK in sustaining journal-ranking systems. These institutions and apparatuses are status-quo-biased, and reinforce social and theoretical stratification in the profession. Together, they reflect the famous Matthew effect: the rich get richer and the poor get poorer (from St Matthew), as described by sociologist Robert Merton.

In the overall dynamic, research from top institutions only goes to top journals, top journals only publish research from top institutions, and so top journals remain top journals and top institutions remain top institutions. I think that is now the main reflexive structure in economics. It has come about because, in the last 25–30 years, the journal-ranking system has been put forcefully into place for judging how people are promoted, how their research is evaluated, and basically how the profession works.

Looking over this time period from the perspective of economic methodology and the history and philosophy of economics, the main development was the elimination of the history (and philosophy) of economics from most economics departments. At the same time, the main generalist journals in economics ceased to publish history and philosophy of economics research, so that most economists ceased to be exposed to it and increasingly regarded it as irrelevant to the practice of economics. That meant that the way in which economics practises or operates the theory-evidence relationship is no longer an issue of concern in the economics profession. Where does that then leave economic methodology in the economics profession? The history and philosophy of economics judge the adequacy of the profession's economic methodology. Minus those fields' influence, most economists now confuse economic methodology and economic method. The former is the epistemology of economics; the latter concerns the tools of economics, especially econometric method, mathematical modelling, and increasingly experimental method. When method replaces methodology, these tools cease to be evaluated in regard to how well they contribute to knowledge. This means evidence is more and more taken at face value, since there is little reflection on what counts as evidence. I suggest the consequence of this development is that economics is becoming a performative science.

A performative science is one that actively seeks to remake the world—I emphasise 'seeks' because it cannot ultimately be successful—in its own image through policy and institutional design changes that incentivise behaviour to fit the theory. The MacKenzie research that has been discussed here is quite good on performativity in connection with the efficient markets hypothesis. Nudge behavioural economics is another example. Its policy recommendation is to alter social structures that incentivize people to behave as rational agents. Mechanism design theory may be even more important, because it aims to design entire market systems in such a way that people must behave as rational choice theory requires in order to be successful. What these initiatives thus do is seek to make the world, or 'perform' it, as standard theory sees it. I see the development of these approaches in mainstream economics as a natural outcome of the marginalisation of economic methodology (and the collapse of methodology into method). Without reflection on the epistemology of economics, economists become insensitive to the nature of the theory-evidence relationship and their role in determining it. Then, they are vulnerable to seeing the world in the image of their own research.

How does this all fit together with the recent emergence of journal-ranking systems as the main means of evaluating research in economics? If you do mainstream research, it is readily identified as such, and so it possesses a self-validating character. In reflexivity terms, mainstream research then functions like a self-fulfilling prophecy. If you do mainstream research, since journal rankings identify this as good research, your research fulfils the requirement of being good research. The opposite is the case with heterodox or non-standard economics. It is a self-defeating prophecy. By being identified as such according to the journal-ranking system, it must go to non-top journals. Since non-top journals only publish lesser quality research, heterodox or non-standard research must be lesser quality research.

So, we have, as one of the outcomes of mainstream economics evolution as a performative science, that it differentiates research practices according to where they originate in a stratified profession. This means many substantive topics are off the table for the mainstream of the profession, not only non-standard research, but such matters as the role of normative values in economics. Another way to put this is to say that economics is becoming an increasingly self-referential science.

I ask, then, is mainstream economics at risk of becoming a bubble science? A science that systematically rebuilds the world and its scientific practice in its own image is one that is likely to fail to explain a changing world. The failure of economics to anticipate and, after the fact, explain the financial crisis fits this picture. A bubble science, then, is one that will suffer significant stranded theoretical asset write-downs. We know from the history of science that this has occurred regularly. There have been many bubble sciences. Marxist economics was mentioned. Is neoclassical economics, its cold war compatriot that played a comparable ideological role, sitting at the end of a similar historical evolution?

It is interesting that mainstream economics seems to have become increasingly performative in a period when other sciences have gained greater influence within economics. I have written fairly extensively about the new movements deriving from other sciences in economics: complexity theory, behavioural economics, experimental strategies, and neuroeconomics. They have all originated from outside of neoclassical economics. Thus, they bring in deep reasoning from other sciences, 'contaminants' by the standards of neoclassical theory, and so we now have an economics ecosystem that is more diffuse and unclear in its overall character. I ask: is there a new reflexivity operating internal to economics generating new methodological and epistemological issues which runs counter to the mainstream's performative ambitions? Might this possible development again require a history and philosophy of economics able to judge economics' recent trajectory relative to its past development? A history and philosophy of economics that takes the present as history?

As a closing remark, let me comment briefly on how mainstream economics might adjust to these other-science influences. One thing that might happen is that key components of standard thinking get replaced piecemeal by new theory components that reflect other-science influences yet still comport with the main thrust of mainstream economics. I take as my example the theory of labour compensation. The standard view is that labour is paid its marginal product. Going back to the 1980s, when game theory and behavioural economics began to influence economics, the Chicago School developed an alternative view of labour compensation called 'tournament theory'. You are no longer rewarded according to your marginal contribution but, rather, according to your success in a lottery among many equally qualified people. Successful individuals then gain employment and income, and are set apart in terms of rank and position appropriate to a stratified world. Lazear and others have shown how labour markets are efficient under this system. So, the old neoclassical marginal reward analysis is put aside, but a mainstream competitive, efficiency-based account is preserved.

Interestingly, an economics that evolved in this way would be less bubble-like because it captures the real world phenomena of social stratification. It does so, on the view suggested here, because it accommodates other-science influences, albeit within its own traditional framework of competition and efficiency. I leave further reflection on this case to other occasions. What seems fair to conclude here, however, is that this kind of evolution of economics works quite well in a world in which a bureaucratic journal-ranking system explains how the science of economics operates.

References

Atkinson, A. B. (1998). *Poverty in Europe*. Oxford: Basil Blackwell. http://eu. wiley.com/WileyCDA/WileyTitle/productCd-0631209093.html

Deaton, A. (2001). Counting the world's poor. *World Bank Research Observer, 16*, 125–147.

MacKenzie, D., & Millo, Y. (2003, July). Constructing a market, performing theory: The historical sociology of a financial derivatives exchange. *American Journal of Sociology, 109*(1), 107–145, 122.

Popper, K. (2013). Science: Conjectures and refutations. In A. Bird & J. Ladyman (Eds.), *Arguing about Science* (p. 16). Abingdon, Oxon: Routledge.

Part II

Case Studies

5

The Keynesian Revolution and the Theory of Countervailing Powers

Robert Skidelsky and Roger Backhouse

The Keynesian Revolution and the Theory of Countervailing Powers by Robert Skidelsky

John Maynard Keynes keeps returning, like an ageing diva giving farewell performances. What does this tell us? First, that in economics there are no final victories or defeats; rather, there are ebbs and flows obedient to changes in consciousness and the world. Second, it tells us that the world changes and so do the structures of power. The rise and fall of different schools of economics is related, undoubtedly, to shifts in the balance of social and economic power. Marx understood that. I want to consider the passage of Keynes' ideas from acceptance to rejection to the modest revival of 2008–2009.

Keynes himself had a distinctive view on these matters. He believed that, soon or late, true ideas will triumph over vested interests. That is

R. Skidelsky (✉)
University of Warwick, Warwickshire, UK

R. Backhouse
University of Birmingham, Birmingham, UK

© The Editor(s) (if applicable) and The Author(s) 2016
R. Skidelsky, N. Craig (eds.), *Who Runs the Economy?*,
DOI 10.1057/978-1-137-58017-7_5

the scientist's faith, but economics is not a natural science. No economic ideas are universally true. That is, we cannot assume that in economics the objects of thought and human societies remain unchanging. I am contrasting that implicitly with natural science, and I now realise that may not be right for the natural sciences either. What I want to argue is that the acceptability of Keynes' ideas varied with their political utility; their truth content has always been contextual.

To be a Keynesian, to state it very baldly, is to want one kind of society rather than another. It is not just a matter of technical analysis, of how economics works. That technical analysis is in service of some larger idea. Before Keynes, policy-makers confronted roughly two choices on how to deal with persisting mass unemployment, both choices having a common root in the maladjustment of supply to demand. The first, suggested by classical economics and endorsed by the political right, explained mass unemployment in terms of the failure of the labour supply to adapt to shifts in demand. For example, if, in the 1920s, coal miners been prepared to accept a wage cut, there need have been no unemployment in coal-mining. Alternatively, if there was a permanently loss of demand for coal, miners—or, at least, their children—should look for jobs as, say, gardeners or bakers and not hang around the coalfields.

The underlying idea, derived from Ricardo—though no longer expressed as crudely as this—, was there was a fixed wages fund for employing labour. If this was used up by three-quarters of the workforce, then one-quarter would be out of work. Why had labour-market flexibility disappeared? The popular explanation of the political right was because of trade union power and welfare benefits. That was very common in the debate on the Great Depression. The left wing took over the idea of a fixed wages fund, though they dressed it up in the Marxist language of exploitation. Unemployment was the direct result of the increased wage and therefore decreased profit share in the national income. Trade unions and government intervention were destroying capitalism's ability to exploit the worker. The capitalist therefore needed a reserve army of the unemployed to maintain his profit rate, though this shrank the market for his products, one of the many contradictions that Marxists discern in the working of the system.

Consider what a policy to combat unemployment based on this kind of analysis would mean. It committed politicians to fighting the class war.

On the one side, it meant destroying or at least weakening trade unions and restricting tax-funded alternatives to work. On the other side, it implied a revolutionary assault on the capitalist system. In most western democracies, there was no political support for carrying either solution to extremes. This left a blocked system with heavy unemployment likely to develop and persist after a shock. The balance of forces was such that no outright victory was possible in the class war. Equally, there was no intellectual foundation for a middle way.

This is, in essence, what the Keynesian revolution provided. On 1 January 1935, Keynes wrote to Bernard Shaw:

> To understand my state of mind, you have to know that I believe myself to be writing a book on economic theory which will largely revolutionise the way the world thinks about economic problems. In particular, the Ricardian foundations of Marxism will be knocked away.

Keynes' overthrow of the Ricardian foundations consisted in the claim that production and employment could be limited not by inefficiency of supply, but by deficiency of demand and, in most circumstances, particularly when unemployment was heavy, output and employment could be boosted by government action to increase total demand.

In America, Kenneth Galbraith's *American Capitalism—The Concept of Countervailing Power* (1952) shows how what he calls the Keynesian formula fitted the rather different structure of the American economy. Galbraith's American economy was dominated by oligopolistic companies. By their ability to set prices above costs, oligopolistic firms provided less employment than competitive firms. In turn, they beget countervailing power in the form of retail organisations, labour unions, and government price regulation schemes, which in aggregate made the economy much more flexible than it was before. Keynes showed—and I am now paraphrasing Galbraith's book—that in such conditions Say's law, that supply always creates its own demand, was invalid. To regain the conditions of full employment by anti-trust legislation—that is, breaking up the oligopolies—was impractical and there was no political support for socialism or public ownership. The Keynesian form of government action to stimulate aggregate demand provided an escape from this dilemma. Galbraith's was an American version of Keynes' suited to oligopolistic competition and administered prices. That was one important strand in the American acceptance of Keynesianism; it was not the only one.

Although Keynes' theory undercut the case for socialism, it did open up the road for government management of the macroeconomy to ensure conditions of optimal equilibrium. There would be no government interference—this was one of its virtues—with managerial prerogatives or decision-making. The government's task was to guarantee full employment. The attainment of full employment of potential resources would be good for both profits and wages. The economy was inside its production possibility frontier. When the problem was one of unused capacity, redistribution was a minor matter. You had some way to go before distribution became an urgent issue.

Such a theory, I suggest, could only have become the basis of policy under conditions of social balance. Keynes' economics was the economics of the middle way, the best that liberal capital could expect in a world veering towards political extremes. However, his economics threw little light on what would happen to class shares of wages and profits when his own policies achieved full employment in conditions of strong union organisation. In such a situation, would the government—or employers—need to recreate Marx's reserve of the unemployed by resisting trade union wage demands or would governments be forced to inflate to keep profits racing ahead of wages? The latter is what Jacob Viner assumed would happen when society got accustomed to full employment. Keynes himself admitted that he had no solution to the wages problem in a full-employment economy. Marxists, too, believed that attempts to overcome the class struggle by inflation would bring only temporary relief.

As we know, Keynesianism dominated the political economy of the developed world from roughly the 1950s through to the middle of the 1970s. As Thomas Palley—to whom I owe much of this section—put it in his 2012 book *From Financial Crisis to Stagnation*,

> Before 1980, economic policy was designed to achieve full employment and the economy was characterised by a system in which wages grew with productivity. This configuration created a virtuous circle of growth. Rising wages meant robust aggregate demand, which contributed to full employment. Full employment in turn provided an incentive to invest, which raised productivity, thereby supporting higher wages.

But, after 1980, a new economic paradigm established itself based on

asset price inflation (equities and housing); widening income inequality; detachment of worker wages from productivity growth; rising household and corporate leverage ratios measured respectively in debt/income and debt/equity ratios; a strong dollar; trade deficits; disinflation or low inflation; and manufacturing job losses.[1]

Workers were pressured on four sides: by globalisation, reduction in the size of government, increase of labour market flexibility, and retreat from full employment. With the membership and influence of trade unions sharply reduced and government weakened, the countervailing power structure, which Galbraith had described in his book, evaporated. Business became the sole prevailing power.

What accounts for this radical shift in ideas and policies? Part of the explanation is almost too obvious: we are never content with what we have. With the achievement of full employment and vigorous growth under the Keynesian aegis, it became easy to forget what life had been before Keynes. It became natural to assume that full employment was the normal state and forget that it was achieved by conscious design. This is the forgetfulness, the amnesia that then followed. Because full employment was there for 20 years, the theory that it was normal for it to be there then revived. The ills of the market were forgotten: it was the ills of government which commanded attention. In economic theory terms, this meant shifting attention from the problem of insufficient demand to the problem of inefficient supply—a return, that is, to the classical agenda of economics.

More specifically, the key reasons for the shift—though these are not exhaustive and should not be considered in isolation from each other—now follow.

On the intellectual side, we got the rehabilitation of the market and the denigration of the state. One can tell the fall of Keynesianism as a purely intellectual story, a counter-revolution in economics, starting with Friedman and adaptive expectations, and ending with the new classical and rational expectations, real business theory, efficient

---

[1] Palley (2012).

financial market theory, and so on. The upshot was a mathematical reinstatement of the classical theory of the self-regulating market. The rehabilitation of the market did not entirely depend on new classical models. There has been a notable revival of Schumpeterian models since the 1980s: capitalism depended on creative destruction, heroic entrepreneurs. In this Promethean perspective, too much stability destroys capitalism's dynamic, so we must learn to ride the surf. Coupled with this was the justification of super-profits as reward for super-enterprise. Right-wing think-tanks and journalists simplified and popularised the academic celebration of markets and revulsion against big government.

One should also notice two other strands feeding into this intellectual counter-revolution: the Austrian theory, which praised markets as sources of decentralised knowledge unavailable to central planners, the theory of public choice, which aimed to show that politicians, far from seeking to achieve the public good, aimed solely to maximise their votes. All the intellectual currents associated with the performance of government and the role of government turned 'right-wing' about this time.

Second, there was Keynesianism's failure to resolve the Ricardo-Marx problem. Keynesian policy created the full-employment economy which the classical economists had assumed was normal. In such an economy, as both Ricardo and Marx had pointed out, there was a unique rate of profit compatible with equilibrium. The neo-Ricardians, indeed, had explained interwar unemployment in terms of the encroachment of wages on profits. What happened later on was that, in the 1970s, Keynesian governments resorted to inflation as a 'vent for social conflict', to use the felicitous phrase of Fred Hirsch. First, they used inflation to suppress a rise in unemployment and then resorted to incomes policy to suppress inflation. Behind the increase in the quantity of money was the conflict between classes for income shares; behind incomes policy, the aim of restoring the profit share. The result was stagflation and a collapse of the existing macro-model. The failure of the Keynesian managers in the 1980s to prevent the encroachment of wages on capital in the full employment, unionised economy they had created, destroyed the political utility of Keynesian economics, and paved the way for the counter-revolution in policy. The theoretical language of monetarism provided anti-Keynesians with the intellectual cover to pursue a policy of destroying union control over the wage bargain. This, from a political economy point of view, is what happened in the 1980s.

The third element in the story was the political shift against trade unions. The lack of a good theory relating employment to prices, the big weakness in the Keynesian political economy, meant that governments in the 1960s and 1970s relied on a social contract with the unions to achieve their over-full employment targets. This not only led to stagflation, as described by Friedman, but, by increasing the monopoly power of organised labour, it turned people against trade unions—even their own members. Unions, in Great Britain at least, threatened to become the prevailing power. If you look at Labour government programmes in the 1970s, they envisaged an economy run by the government and the trade unions with a decreasing role for private business. Thatcherism was the political reaction to that.

The change in the structure of the economy is obviously very central to this story. How much of this was due to autonomous technological innovation and how much due to policies to restore profits? I know of no good theory which endogenizes technological change. However, two structural changes seem to be key: the consolidation of big business and banking, and the shift to a service economy. In the much enlarged financial sector, the degree of concentration has increased enormously: for example, five banks control 80% of UK lending. We were told we were creating competitive markets—whereas, in fact, we were creating a global network of financial oligopolies.

What about globalisation, This may be interpreted as the effort of business to escape national regulation. It was based on the export of manufacturing jobs where unions were strong and rebuilding the economy on the basis of service jobs where they were weak. Globalisation was the business response to the declining rate of profit. Globalisation was seen as the master key to the overall improvement in the position of the business class. It increased corporate profits, reduced prices of consumer goods, and made possible a huge influx of outside money—of course, eventually, from East Asia—into the western banking system. However, most importantly, it was used as a bludgeon to frighten workers and to emasculate their economic power.

One consequence of the new paradigm is that the welfare state as the basis of the social contract was replaced by access to credit. This is a point that many have made—and Thomas Palley has made it most explicitly. Because the new social contract was based on access to cheap credit, the economy built on credit became increasingly unsustainable. No real assets were being created for much of it and therefore it was bound to collapse. It will collapse again.

Prospects of a revival of Keynesianism depend on its future political utility. That is the onus of my argument. Keynes was brought out of the cupboard when the world economy crashed in 2008 but then largely put back after a few months when stimulus policies had done their job of limiting the damage.

What about the future? The question is whether we can afford to go along with a system that crashes every few years with increasingly serious social consequences. It is probably impossible, as well as undesirable, to restore the trade unions as a countervailing power. I am not so sure about the 'undesirable' but, in the kind of economy we have, I do not see how it could be done: that is, in an economy dominated by banks, the service sector, and high-tech manufacturing. You have the alternative idea of breaking up the concentrations of banks. That kind of anti-trust way of restoring capitalism to health is probably unavailable in the increasingly integrated global market we have.

A popular uprising against the system is possible, but the political extremes are ideologically threadbare, unlike in the 1920s and 1930s. That leaves the state as the only possible countervailing power. It can be argued that national states cannot control global capital and that a world state is unavailable, but a 'single world' model of globalisation is not the only one. One might think of global integration developing along regional lines. This offers a more feasible route to reinserting democratic oversight of the economy.

The Eurozone is not a particularly brilliant example. It shows how difficult it is to transfer democratic accountability beyond the bounds of a nation state. But a reformed Eurozone, one with a proper central bank and Treasury, could, in principle, re-write the social contract on behalf of its weaker members. That is the best we have any right to expect.

The Keynesian Revolution and the Theory of Countervailing Powers by Roger Backhouse

I am not going to take forward the story told by Robert Skidelsky, because it would be difficult to match the breadth of his discussion. Instead, I am going to go back in time, to the 1930s, and retell the story of the Keynesian revolution in the USA. Doing this adds some of the important background. Galbraith has been mentioned and his work links to a very significant strand of thinking in the USA of the 1930s that is usually overlooked. When you read the economic literature from the Great Depression, you find quotation after quotation that resonates with today, talking about the power of business, inequality, the effects of inequality on demand, and so on. I would like to read some of these quotations, but I am conscious of our time constraint.

I suggest we focus on the American literature of the 1930s. In claiming this, I am not challenging what Robert has said. His story is very much the Keynesian revolution from the point of view of Britain and Keynes. My point is that, although there were close connections, the experiences of the USA and Britain were not the same, either in terms of long-term economic trajectories or the immediate experience in the interwar period. In Britain, after the immediate cycle at the end of World War I, there was a period of stagnation. This is when all the factors that Robert talked about become very important: the unions, uncompetitiveness due to high wages, and so on. This is the background, I would suggest, to the British experience of the Great Depression.

In the USA, things are completely different. The frontier played an important role in the history of the USA. It was part of the basis for America being different from the rest of the world, because its economy could develop in a different way. That came into the story in the 1930s. Also, America was the land of the individualist in a way I think Britain probably never was. Laissez-faire had very deep roots in America. Both of these were major factors in how Americans came to respond to the Depression. Also, in the USA in the 1920s, there was a massive boom preceding the collapse. The 1920s were a complete contrast in the two countries. In the USA, it was possible to think of the depression as a business cycle that had somehow gone catastrophically wrong.

How did America respond? The dominant view in the literature—my paper 'Economic Power and the Financial Machine: Competing Conceptions of Market Failure in the Great Depression', forthcoming in *History of Political Economy*, discusses this in great detail—was to say, 'What has happened is the competitive free-market system has simply broken down.' Diagnoses of the Depression such as you find in the proceedings of the American Economic Association conferences in the early 1930s or the series of volumes coming out of the Brookings Institution and other places, were that competition had broken down. The reason for the Depression was market power. Now, this is different from simply saying that prices or wages are rigid, perhaps because of the power of unions. The argument is that business plays a role in the economy which involves prices inducing structural change, and things like that, and the concentration of business power has messed this up. It is a different perspective from that one finds in Britain. What had happened was that economic power had become really concentrated and this was the problem. You had monopoly and oligopoly, and it had caused the economic system to break down.

I have tried to document all of these reasons why economic power was seen as crucial to the Depression. This, I think, gives a different slant on the Keynesian revolution. In my paper, the way I tried to sort it out was by focusing on the activities of what was a major event at the time: the Temporary National Economic Committee (TNEC), which was meeting in 1938–1941. I quote from the letter from Roosevelt to Congress on 29 April 1938 in which he asked for this Committee to be set up:

> Among us today a concentration of private power without equal in history is growing. This concentration is seriously impairing the economic effectiveness of private enterprise as a way of providing employment for labor [sic] and capital and as a way of assuring a more equitable distribution of income and earnings among the people of the nation as a whole.

Over next 2 to 3 years, monographs were produced and the Committee met to take testimony from witness after witness. According to George Stigler's count, 33,000 pages of reports and evidence were produced.

Most of this was on precisely that theme: what has happened to the concentration of industry, the concentration of wealth, and the concentration of ownership of everything? How has that caused a breakdown? This, I would suggest, is fairly central to the American understanding of the Depression in the 1930s.

How does Keynesianism come into this? Two of the witnesses who were called were Alvin Hansen and Lauchlin Currie. Other people have told the story about how they turned up and wowed the committee with their Keynesian ideas. Despite their testimony covering only 88 pages out of those 33,000 pages, that is what many people have remembered. What they argued was that what had happened was not a problem with economic power but that the 'financial machine' had gone wrong. Again, this is a difference from Britain. I have not had time to think about this—and maybe Robert might have things to say on this because, if you look back to Keynes in 1914 or thereabouts, I think he is talking about the power in financial markets and thinking about power in the financial machine. At this time, Hansen and Currie were putting forward Keynesianism as a technical device involving flows of funds. Economic power is not mentioned in their discussions or their testimony, or in the papers they wrote.

To bowdlerise the story, in a sense their Keynesian revolution was almost converting the dialogue from a discussion of economic power to a discussion of the technicalities of financial flows and how financial flows led to investment. The idea was that the machine had broken down and therefore savings were not getting translated into investment.

Now, although Currie and Hansen were presenting a technical argument, politics was not far away. What happens on the day that Currie and Hansen were giving their testimony? Roosevelt writes another letter to the Committee. I think they read this out over lunchtime after one session. In it, he explained that he was concerned not only with idle men in factories, but also with the vast reservoir of money and savings that had remained idle in stagnant pools. So, on the day they were testifying before the Committee—and this was surely not coincidence, given that Currie was in the White House—a letter comes from Roosevelt to the Committee saying, 'This is what you have to consider.'

In a sense, this is distracting attention from economic power. When the report was written up, the person who was writing up the report brought the two together and talked, almost in a Hobsonian manner, about concentration of wealth being one of the reasons the financial machine had got clogged up. This, I hope, is enough to justify my claim that, though this event may seem rather remote, the discussions covered inequality, and concentration of power within corporations, in a way that has become topical again.

These events also help to explain modern Keynesianism. I have in mind not just Kenneth Galbraith, but also Paul Samuelson, who wrote the dominant textbook used to teach economics in the 1950s and onwards. If you are thinking about post-war Keynesianism, you have to understand Paul Samuelson. If you read his 1948 textbook, you find him quoting from the proceedings of the TNEC on the structure of industry. 'We have this theory of competitive markets—now let us think about what business is really like', and he gives an account that would be acceptable to many of the economists from the 1930s I have been talking about. This is not the standard neoclassical account of how businesses really work.

There was a certain degree of pluralism in post-war Keynesianism, even in the dominant textbook of this period. There is neoclassical theory; but there are also ideas from the institutionalist critique of big business in the 1930s. Rooting Keynesianism in this context also helps explain the extreme animus that big business—or certain strands of it—had to Keynesian economics. Keynesian economics was associated not just with the New Deal, but also with a critique or sustained attack on economic power, because it is part of the TNEC report, which is clearly an attack on business. In the 1930s, a group of businessmen, focused on the Dupont company, started organising opposition to the New Deal, and along came Keynesian economics as part of this whole package they are opposing. This hostility to the New Deal got translated into hostility to Samuelson's textbook.

Keynesian economics could never be taken as something neutral, technical, and purely scientific. Because people were so vehemently opposed to the New Deal, because it infringed on Dupont's ability to do what it wanted—and they could also present it as infringing the traditional American views about laissez-faire—Keynesianism was tainted, even if some of the Keynesians had tried to distance themselves from the notion that economic power was the problem.

Reference

Palley, T. (2012). *From financial crisis to stagnation*. Cambridge: Cambridge University Press.

6

The Neoclassical Counter-Revolution and the Ascendancy of Business

Daniel Stedman Jones and Ben Jackson

The Neoclassical Counter-Revolution and the Ascendancy of Business by Daniel Stedman Jones

The resurgence of neoclassical free market ideas in the middle of the twentieth century can be located in the transatlantic rise and development of neoliberal politics. 'Neoliberal' is not a straightforward term and requires some explanation. Neoliberalism was a movement of economists and liberal critics led by an Austrian professor of economics, Friedrich Hayek, who sought a middle way between the night watchman state of nineteenth-century laissez-faire and the rejection of the market characteristic of totalitarianism of right and left. But neoliberalism underwent a transformation in the course of the 1930s–1970s, a shift which laid the ground for the political success of some of its central ideas.

D.S. Jones (✉)
39 Essex Chambers, London, UK

B. Jackson
University of Oxford, Oxford, UK

© The Editor(s) (if applicable) and The Author(s) 2016
R. Skidelsky, N. Craig (eds.), *Who Runs the Economy?*,
DOI 10.1057/978-1-137-58017-7_6

73

The intellectual trajectory of neoliberal politics began with Hayek's critique of Keynes in the 1930s when based at the London School of Economics (LSE), and flowered with his later establishment of the Mont Pelerin Society (MPS) in 1947. The MPS was (and is) an international network of self-styled 'classical liberals' who challenged the rise of Keynesianism. More broadly, the MPS neoliberals attacked 'collectivism', which they saw in the social and liberal democracy of Franklin D. Roosevelt's New Deal and the post-war Labour government as much as in Stalin's Russia.

The initial group around Hayek can be properly characterised as neoliberal; they called themselves 'neoliberals'. Hayek called himself a neoliberal—as did his European friends, who were dotted around Europe and the USA, at the LSE in London, in Paris, in Freiburg in Germany, in Switzerland, and in Chicago. The Chicago economist Frank Knight was also a member and his colleague Henry Simons was instrumental in early discussions with Hayek about the putative organisation before his untimely death in 1946. Both developed a similar set of ideas about the need to protect the market system at the same time as developing social protections to combat mass unemployment and economic depression. They, too, can be characterised as neoliberal in this early sense, although they did not call themselves neoliberals in the same way that Hayek and the German social-market theorists did.

In the post-war period, neoliberalism was radicalised in the USA. The centre of gravity of neoliberal ideas moved across the Atlantic from Europe in the work of the economists and theorists of the Chicago School of Economics and the Virginia School of Political Economy. Though the key figures—Milton Friedman, George Stigler, James Buchanan, and Gordon Tullock—were all involved with the MPS in its early days, they stopped referring to themselves as neoliberal by the 1950s. (The term then seems to disappear until re-emerging more recently in the work of social scientists and, especially, critics of globalisation.)

Chicago and Virginia theorists were crucially important because, from the 1950s onwards, they advocated untrammelled free markets, combining both a neoclassical framework and the insights of Keynesian macroeconomics. The revolutionary nature of these ideas was their astonishing reach. No arena or issue was felt to be immune from market-based analysis. Along with Hayek's critique of planning, proposals for market liberalisation, deregulation, monetarism, and the introduction of public choice models to government administration and public services broke through politically in the 1970s in Britain and the USA. In particular, three different dimensions can be drawn from this economic movement, each of which relate specifically to economics and power.

The first dimension was the Chicago and Virginia critique, developed cumulatively, of political power and the proper balance or limits between the market, on the one hand, and the state, on the other. The second, also discussed by Ben Jackson in his contribution on the Institute of Economic Affairs (IEA), was Hayek's intellectual strategy for political influence, which Milton Friedman in particular perfected. Hayek drew on British Fabian socialism as a model of ideas that percolated slowly and enduringly, through think-tanks, policy expertise and journalism, to political power. The third, linked, dimension is the complicated observable relationship between economic ideas and economic policy since the 1970s, which reveals much about economics and power.

In terms of the neoliberal critique, the American Chicago and Virginia neoliberals developed a multi-faceted assault on received notions of political power. I have discussed the importance of monetarism, privatisation, and trickle-down economics elsewhere.[1] Here, the emphasis is on several other elements of what is often called the 'neoclassical counter-revolution'.

First, there is the shift from an idea about the importance of ex ante regulation held by early neoliberals—and, especially, the social-market theorists—to deregulation, advocated by Stigler in particular. American neoliberal theorists changed from understanding regulation as a process by which competition could be sustained and enhanced to a conviction that government was the problem and should be removed altogether. This transformation is an important case study of the change in neoliberalism in the post-war years. As historians like Robert Van Horn have shown, deregulation emerged from a particular constellation of intellectual and corporate influences in 1950s Chicago.[2]

---

[1] See *Masters*, especially Chaps. 5 and 6.
[2] Van Horn (2009).

Second, the Virginia public choice critique denied the possibility of an objective public interest embodied by the publically-spirited or fair-minded public official or civil servant on the model of Beveridge or Keynes. Ronald Coase, in his article 'The Problem of Social Cost' (1960), pointed to the limits of fair spirited public intervention, which dovetailed with Stigler's theories on economic regulation. Buchanan and Tullock introduced public choice, the application of a Madisonian checks-and-balances approach across bureaucracies and government administration, in their book *The Calculus of Consent* (1962) and in Buchanan's later ideas about constitutional economics.

Third, American neoliberalism embarked on what has been called, pejoratively, 'economics imperialism'. This is the movement led in Chicago by Gary Becker, but of which Virginia public choice also forms a central part. Becker applied a neoclassical framework to all areas of social life, developing the idea of choice units operating in a market environment. No area was to be immune from colonisation by economic market-based analysis. The family, crime, drugs, as well as politics, the constitution or the state could be explained—in Becker's models, but also in those of Buchanan, Tullock or Stigler—in economic terms.

In each of these areas, and cumulatively, it is possible to see the build-up of a fundamental and destructive critique of social democracy—and 'social democracy' in this context included, though there were important differences, the liberal democracy in the USA of Roosevelt's New Deal. The neoliberal attack undermined the key parts of the mid-twentieth-century welfare state and its allied assumptions about economic management: the pursuit of full employment, economic planning and regulation, and the welfare state.

It is noteworthy that the comprehensive nature of the attack mounted by American neoliberalism relied, in part, for its success on a particular choice of measures by which its success could then be assessed. This is very telling in the context of how economics, and its successes or failures, might relate to those in power. Famously, Friedman and his critics debated the data and analysis he and Anna Jacobsen Schwartz produced in their *Monetary History of the United States* (1965), which formed the bedrock of Friedman's claims that the Federal Reserve System had caused the Great Depression. The phenomenon can also be illustrated by a remarkable quote from Buchanan in a paper from 1954. Buchanan talks about political power and economic power—or, rather, individual power and economic freedom—and says:

> The essential point to be emphasised in this connection is that the inequalities present in market choice are inequalities in individual power and not in individual freedom, if care is taken to define freedom and power in such a way as to maximise the usefulness of these two concepts in discussion. As [Frank] Knight has suggested, it seems desirable for this reason to define freedom somewhat narrowly as the absence of coercion and unfreedom as the state of being prevented from utilising the normally available capacities for action.[3]

Buchanan's quote is interesting because it encapsulates a feature of the neoliberal endeavour. It combines aspects of the American neoliberal critique. Buchanan wants to make claims about values and, in particular, about freedom, on the one hand, but also wants to limit the terms used to discuss concepts like freedom in such a way as to factor out certain things that are harder to measure in non-economic, or non-market, terms. Freedom must be measured in terms of negative freedom, which clearly echoes a very important philosophical debate. Elsewhere in the article Buchanan accepts there are other types of value which the market cannot measure.[4] Coase says something similar in 'The Problem of Social Cost: 'the choice between different social arrangements for the solution of economic problems should be carried out in broader terms than' just those 'measured by the market'.[5] These writers enter into the arena of freedom, but they also want to limit the way it is defined, discussed, and measured.

The second dimension of neoliberalism's contribution to the neoclassical counter-revolution is the focus provided by Hayek and Friedman on the importance of a transatlantic, indeed global, political network and a model of change, and the influence of economics on political power. Hayek consciously emulated the Fabian socialists' foundation of the LSE and the Fabian Society. He admired the impact of progressive thought in the early twentieth century. Before Kuhn, he understood the importance

---

[3] Buchanan (1954).
[4] Ibid., p. 341.
[5] Coase (1960).

of paradigms. In his article 'The Intellectuals and Socialism' (1949), Hayek set out very clearly a desire to influence intellectuals, who he considered to be a very wide group:

> The class [of intellectuals] does not consist of only journalists, teachers, ministers, lecturers, publicists, radio commentators, writers of fiction, cartoonists, and artists all of whom may be masters of the technique of conveying ideas but are usually amateurs so far as the substance of what they convey is concerned. The class also includes many professional men and technicians, such as scientists and doctors, who through their habitual intercourse with the printed word become carriers of new ideas outside their own fields and who, because of their expert knowledge of their own subjects, are listened to with respect on most others. There is little that the ordinary man of today learns about events or ideas except through the medium of this class.[6]

As this passage makes clear, Hayek envisaged a (perhaps) relatively dated idea about the importance of the elite. However, that model was successfully followed by neoliberal activists, especially by the public intellectual par excellence, Milton Friedman, and by various think-tanks in American and Britain. The first wave of think-tanks emerged in the 1940s and 1950s with the American Enterprise Institute, the Foundation for Economic Education, and the British IEA. A second wave followed in the 1970s with the establishment of the Heritage Foundation, the Cato Institute and, in Britain, the Centre for Policy Studies and the Adam Smith Institute.

The neoliberal influence, like that of the Fabians before them, provides an interesting case study of a particular model of change. It begs the question of whether we are in the midst of a similar or different model now. Is there a countervailing theory that is being promoted elsewhere, or that will emerge or come through different think-tanks or other organisations? Is that model no longer replicable in an age characterised by the widespread availability of information and critique made possible by the internet?

The third dimension of the neoclassical counter-revolution is the actual or potential influence of economic ideas. How do economic ideas influence politics? Are economic policies more reflective of changes in economic conditions and changed structures than of economic ideas? In the

---

[6] Hayek (1949).

early twentieth century, Keynes' ideas—in the economic desperation of the interwar period—arguably meshed with the flowering of the state. In the late nineteenth century and early twentieth century, there was a huge expansion in administrative capacity and institutional responsibility, and the growth of new interests aligned with those developments. Keynes' ideas emerged at the same time, offering a way for this institutional configuration of economics and power to be directed in a particular policy direction.

In the 1970s, there was a different configuration shaped by the breakdown of many of the prevailing global economic certainties. The collapse of Bretton Woods, the recurrent oil crises, and the appearance of 'stagflation' combined to demand new policy responses. Friedman himself accepted that it was events which largely drove the application of his ideas. It was not so much that they could be considered to be leaders but, rather, that their ideas were available and they seemed to offer an alternative where other ideas had broken down or failed. This was clearly apparent in the approaches of policy-makers and officials in the 1970s. It has not yet been witnessed so clearly since 2008. A brief Keynesian resurgence occurred in 2008–2009 before the politics of austerity dominated. No clear alternative or new paradigm has emerged.

Observation of the economic policy shifts of the last century leads to two paradoxical conclusions. The first is that ideas do matter. They matter not least because, even if new economic ideas manifested in economic policy reflect structural change rather than heroic inspiration, their effects once a new approach is adopted still result in cultural changes in institutions. It will be recognisable to policy experts of all stripes that, since the late 1980s, it has been a reflex in government and the civil service to say, 'We must have a market solution. We must find it and apply it.' That can be done in an unthinking way but it is a clear illustration of the fact that, whatever the precise cause or relationship in the 1970s, the lasting impact of a new set of ideas really did transform policy-making. As Hayek understood, the paradigm changed.

The second conclusion is that the clearest producers of political disruption are actual economic events. Ideas reflect those events as much as shape them. Economic crises drive political and economic change through the inapplicability of existing economic paradigms to specific problems, which must nevertheless be addressed by economic policy. In this sense, economic history is probably a better guide than economic theory, especially of a purportedly predictive kind.

The Neoclassical Counter-Revolution and the Ascendancy of Business by Ben Jackson

Daniel Stedman Jones has given us a panoramic view of the rise of the free-market right. I am going to follow that by saying something smaller and more parochial, focusing on the case of Britain. It picks up not only on what Daniel has said, but also on some of the points that Norbert and Robert made earlier in this volume about the way in which interests interact with, and sponsor, certain kinds of economic ideas. In particular, I have done some work recently on the Institute of Economic Affairs (IEA), a think-tank that is clearly one of the central institutions in the story of the rise of free-market politics in Britain.[7] I therefore examine what the case study of the IEA tells us about how power and the ideas of the New Right intersect each other. I make three brief points.

The first point to some extent echoes what Daniel has said about the political strategy of the IEA. The key figures in the IEA explicitly drew their political analysis from the article by Hayek that Daniel mentioned— 'The Intellectuals and Socialism' (1949)—which argued that political feasibility was determined by a kind of conventional wisdom that was itself the product of what Hayek called 'second-hand dealers in ideas'—that is, the long list of characters that Daniel mentioned, including writers, journalists, teachers, cartoonists and so on. These are the sort of characters who Hayek thought formed the conventional policy wisdom. These individuals did not necessarily have any particular claim to expertise themselves, but they drew on what they took to be the most fashionable expert opinions and then they broadcast them to a wider audience. The key to changing policy, then, on this analysis, was to change the minds of his opinion-forming stratum of society. From this perspective, the institution of the think-tank was a crucial one, because it changed the climate of opinion by persuading journalists and politicians that what they had

---

[7] For a longer version of the argument presented here, see Jackson, 2012.

previously regarded as intellectually unfashionable was, on the contrary, at the cutting edge of political thinking.

Obviously, there is a 'battle of ideas' element to that story, but, as a number of scholars have pointed out when they looked at that narrative in more detail, we should not analyse that story purely in idealist terms. Free-market ideas did not obtain prominence solely because of the incisive writing of great minds, but because of a concerted effort that was sponsored by a sympathetic business elite to disseminate these ideas through an international network of interlocking institutions. The IEA was an important British manifestation of that wider effort.

The literature on the IEA often presents it as changing policy through a long-run process of change. The story is that they bombarded university students, school-teachers and university lecturers with publications in a bid to shift the teaching of economics and politics to the next generation in their favoured ideological direction. The IEA was not, in practice, particularly successful in persuading educationalists to shift to the right, but they stumbled instead on an alternative and more effective strategy, which was influencing the views of the small media and political elite that shaped public policy debate in Britain. That was a job that was particularly easy to pull off in the small, closed world of the political elite in Britain in the 1960s and 1970s. The IEA ended up narrowing its sights on a subset of the second-hand dealers in ideas by zeroing in on the media and political elite.

My second point is that, as I have already mentioned, there were important material foundations to the success of this advocacy. There has been a great deal of academic and political discussion about the financing of free-market ideas in the USA, focusing on the links between business organisations and the right's intellectual infrastructure. Not as much work has been done on the relationship between the diffusion of free-market ideas in Britain and their sponsors in the business community, but organisations like the IEA were only able to operate successfully because of donations from business. Their other sources of revenue were never enough to cover their costs.

Of course, we do not necessarily want to make a straightforward materialist point about the payer of the piper calling the tune, because it is perhaps more accurate to say that there was a kind of mutual influence between organisations like the IEA and their funders. The fund-raising efforts of the IEA were simultaneously an exercise in harvesting much needed financial and political support, which inevitably would condition the nature of the work they undertook, but it was also about the IEA teaching the business community what sort of economy and society were in their own best interests.

Famously, the IEA was founded by a businessman, Antony Fisher, and there is a well-known origin myth of the IEA that focuses on Fisher going to see Hayek and Hayek advising Fisher that the best way to make a political impact was to found a think-tank. In much of the literature on the IEA, Fisher is the only source of funding for the IEA that is mentioned. Richard Cockett's book, *Thinking the Unthinkable*, for example, focuses on Fisher's role in funding the IEA. Fisher was indeed wealthy; he made his money by introducing the battery farming of chickens to the British farming industry. However, Fisher's funding was quickly displaced by a larger number of corporate donations. There was a steep rise in corporate donations to the IEA over the course of the 1960s. During the 1970s, there were between 250 and 300 companies regularly giving every year to the IEA. Consistent donors represented a fair cross-section of the business community, including major companies such as BP, Marks & Spencer, Procter & Gamble, Unilever, the high-street banks, newspapers and institutions from the City. Uniquely among British institutions, the IEA found the 1970s to be a time of great financial promise. They did very well in the 1970s, in spite of the adverse economic circumstances, and increased their revenue from corporate donations in real terms.

You can track a change in the IEA's message from its beginnings in 1957 up to the 1980s. As originally presented in the 1950s and 1960s, the IEA's brief was to oppose anti-competitive business practices, as well as ill-advised state interventions; however, by the time you get to the 1970s and 1980s, it is really the problems of government that occupy the IEA's attention and form the core of the fundraising appeals to business. In effect, the IEA presented itself as trying to defend business from the clumsy attention of politicians and trade unions.

The final point I want to make is that while business provided an important resource to help organisations like the IEA function, the second indispensable ingredient to its success was clearly the intellectual authority that was available to them from leading free-market scholars and, especially, the string of Nobel Prize-winning economists who were members of the Mont Pelerin Society, notably Hayek, Milton Friedman, and James Buchanan. In that sense, a purely materialist account would not capture the full complexity of the IEA's success. However, it is interesting to note that these very prestigious scholars who bolstered the intellectual profile of the IEA were all based outside Britain. Many of the major economists were often American or were attached to the American economics profession. There were no British figures of comparable academic eminence who allied themselves with the dissemination of free-market ideas.

British economists certainly made a contribution. There were figures like Peter Bauer and Alan Walters and many others. However, although these figures were important as supporting characters—and, in Alan Walters' case, as an advisor in government—these British economists would not have made the same impact in the absence of the foundations that had been laid by their allies overseas. In this sense, it was the ability to import ideas from the USA and the wider international free-market network that fuelled the IEA's success. This might therefore be viewed as a case study in the Americanisation of British post-war politics—and particularly in the power of the American economics profession to set British agendas in this period.

The more familiar account of the IEA is a story of maverick outsiders who rocked the establishment and fought their way up from the streets, eventually to take over the British state with Thatcher. But, as I have tried to show, that is an overstated and mythological account. A more precise characterisation is that these free-market advocates had only a marginal presence in British universities: they were a small minority among intellectuals and lacked significant support in the British economics profession in the 1960s and 1970s. The heavy intellectual artillery had to be imported from overseas, but there *was* significant indigenous support from business, from the media and, eventually, influential politicians. In that sense, you could say that free-market advocates were insufficiently faithful to their own creed in publicly emphasising the importance of intellectual conversion to their cause. In a politics dominated by private interests, it was skilful marketing that was crucial to securing a dominant position in the marketplace of ideas.

References

Buchanan, J. (1954, August). Individual choice in the market and in voting. *Journal of Political Economy, 62*(4), 340.

Coase, R. (1960, October). The problem of social cost. *Journal of Law and Economics, 3*, 43.

Hayek, F. (1949). The intellectuals and socialism. *University of Chicago Law Review*, (Spring), 418.

Jackson, B. (2012). The think-tank archipelago: Thatcherism and neo-liberalism. In B. Jackson and R. Saunders (eds.), Making Thatcher's Britain. Cambridge: Cambridge University Press.

Van Horn, R. (2009). Reinventing monopoly and the role of corporations: The roots of Chicago law and economics. In P. Mirowski & D. Plehwe (Eds.), *The road from Mont Pelerin*. Cambridge: Harvard University Press.

Part III

Applications to the Present

7

Economics and the Banks

Adair Turner

Economics and the Banks by Adair Turner

My focus is on economics and the banks or, more generally, economics and the whole financial system. And I want to do three things: first, set out some facts about the rising importance of finance within the economy; second, consider what orthodox economics said about the rising importance of finance before the crisis and how what it said turned out to be completely wrong; and third, discuss to what extent the profound mistakes of modern economics reflected the autonomous development of an intellectual tradition and how far, instead, the explanations lie in power relationships.

A. Turner (✉)
Institute for New Economic Thinking, New York, NY, USA

Rising Financial Intensity

There have been several studies of the growth in the relative role of finance within modern economies. One by Andy Haldane[1] found that the size of the US financial system grew from about 2.5 % of GDP in 1950 to 8 % of GDP in 2008. Finance got much bigger in our economies. Another important study by Philippon and Reshef asked how much financiers are paid relative to people of an apparently similar skill level in the rest of the economy.[2] They found that the 1920s, which saw very rapid growth in the relative importance of finance, also saw a large 'excess wage', and they found that that excess wage re-emerged on a very large scale after about the 1980s.

Finance grew very much bigger and it was very well-paid. And we must ask whether that was good for the economy, because finance is different from other sectors. If the restaurant business grew as a proportion of the economy, we would not even ask whether that was good or bad, we would simply say: 'Restaurants have grown in importance because people are choosing to spend an increasing percentage of their income on restaurant meals.' But nobody gets up in the morning and says, 'What will I do today? I think I will buy some financial services for a bit of fun.' Financial services are not forms of end consumption, but perform intermediate functions within the economy. More finance is good if it is making the economy more efficient or more stable, and it is bad if it is making it inefficient and unstable. So, we have to work out what impact it has had.

A key first step is to identify which specific aspects of finance got bigger. A fine study by Robin Greenwood and David Scharfstein of Harvard University helps answer that question.[3] General insurance has grown a little faster than GDP because people's houses are more expensive and they have more things to insure: but there is nothing about the growth of general or life insurance which raises prima facie concerns about stability or efficiency, and insurance has not been a major driver of the dramatic increase in the relative importance of finance within our economies.

---

[1] Haldane (2010).

[2] Philippon and Reshef (2012).

[3] Greenwood and Scharfstein (2013).

Instead, as Greenwood and Scharfstein illustrate, two developments dominate: one is that the finance industry has, over time, made much more money out of the provision of credit—from net interest margin and from fees on credit facilities; the other is that far more money is now made out of the complex nexus of activities which go to make up broadly defined 'asset management'.

It is not surprising that the industry has made ever more money out of credit provision, because there is far more credit extended to the real economy than there was 50 or 60 years ago. In aggregate for the advanced economies, private sector credit as a percentage of GDP went from 50 % in 1950 to 170 % by 2008. There is more credit provided to the real economy, and that means a bigger financial services industry to provide that credit.

Part of the growth of asset management, in turn, is simply the flip side of more credit. If there are more debt liabilities in the economy there must be more financial assets and, in some way or another, those assets will be managed. Some of those will be very straightforward bank deposits, but some of them will be, for instance, money market funds, hedge fund assets, corporate bonds, and mortgage securities. There will be a larger quantity of fixed income assets to be managed—and that, along with increased equity market capitalisation, is part of the story of why asset management (in all it multiple forms) has grown.

But the other reason why the sum of all the activities involved in managing assets has grown is that, in addition to the financial system doing more units of activity vis-à-vis the real economy, it does phenomenally more units of activity *with itself*. For the other striking development of the last 40 years is an explosion of *intra*-financial system activity. Household debt and corporate debt have grown as percentages of GDP, but the most explosive growth of debt over the last 30 years in the USA has been the debts owed by the financial sector to the financial sector; that is, *intra-financial* system assets and liabilities.

That reflects, in part, the development of a securitised credit system, in which credit may be not just held on a bank's balance sheet but may be turned into a credit security. It then may be sold to, for instance, a structured investment vehicle (SIV), which issues asset-backed commercial paper, which is bought by a money market mutual fund: or in which the same bank which had originated and distributed a package of credit securities may, in its trading room, buy them back. As a result, the system came to be built on complicated multi-step chains of credit intermediation: it entailed massively increased trading activity, and its complexity created risks which needed to be managed with derivative contracts—which could also, however, be used to take further yet risky positions.

The dramatic impact of all this on the banking industry can be understood by comparing a major bank balance sheet from the 1960s and one from today. Look at a major bank balance sheet from the 1960s, and even someone with little specialist knowledge of finance could understand it. On the asset side, there were cash, government bonds, and loans to households and corporates; on the liability side, deposits from households or corporates, with a fairly small quantity of inter-bank borrowings as the balancing item. But if you pick up the balance sheet of JP Morgan, Goldman Sachs, RBS or Deutsche Bank today, you will find that over 50 % of it arises from a complex set of assets and liabilities, or derivative contracts owed to and from other banks and other financial institutions: RBS dealing with Deutsche Bank, Deutsche Bank with Morgan Stanley, or Goldman Sachs with hedge funds.

This huge complexity is summed up by a diagram which was produced by the New York Federal Reserve shortly after the crisis, in which they attempted to plot out all of the connections in what we call 'the shadow banking system'. The report which included this chart concluded with a recommendation which said that anybody seeking to understand the system should print out the chart out on a piece of paper measuring three foot by four foot—anything smaller and you cannot see what is going on.

The Pre-crisis Orthodoxy

So, that is what occurred—more credit, more leverage, more fixed income assets to manage, and a huge increase in intra-financial system complexity. What, then, did economics—and public commentary more generally—say about the economic impact of this increasing financial intensity? In terms of rising real economy credit and leverage, it said essentially three things:

The first was that finance theorists gave us a theory of why we need debt instruments as well as equity instruments in our economy. The answer is that contracts which are, to a degree, 'non-state contingent' help overcome the problems of 'costly state verification': if you make an equity investment, you have far less information than the managers of the company about the risks taken and the results received, and the most effective response is therefore often to strike a debt contract which promises you a predefined return not dependent on the results of the underlying real investments.[4] And economic historians, meanwhile, told us that we probably would not have had the industrial revolution if we had tried to finance it all through equity contracts: we needed the possibility of debt contract as well. So, theory and empiricisms together gave us the conclusion seen in meta-studies like Ross Levine's *Handbook of Economic Growth* (2005), which suggested not only that financial deepening is in general good, but specifically that private sector credit as a percentage of GDP is positively correlated with growth and welfare.[5]

Second, there was a tendency to assume that, in some general sense, we *needed* strong credit growth in order to achieve adequate consumption growth, nominal demand growth and, thus, economic growth—a belief which therefore saw growth in consumer credit as being as important as business lending. Here, in fairness, we can largely absolve academic economics of support for this proposition, since academic justifications for rising credit intensity always tended to be focused on lending to business. But those academic arguments, perhaps imperfectly understood, appeared to provide justification for more rapid growth in credit than in nominal GDP. And many regulators accepted it as a given that bank capital requirements had to be set low enough to facilitate strong credit growth for home buyers and consumers as much as for business.

The third proposition of pre-crisis economics, by contrast, was that the details of the financial system and the level of leverage in the economy were simply irrelevant to macroeconomic stability considerations such

---

[4] Townsend (1979).
[5] Levine (2005).

as cyclical stability and the rate of inflation. So that, if you left the finance rooms of the academy and went down the corridor to the modern macro theorists, you entered a realm in which finance could be considered as an unimportant 'veil' through which the impetus of the interest rate passed to affect price and output in the real economy, but without any need to model the details of the banking or wider financial system. Dynamic stochastic general equilibrium (DSGE) models in which representative agent households and representative agent companies struck contracts could therefore capture all that mattered in macro dynamics without providing an account of the banking system. And a book like Michael Woodford's 700-page *Interest and Prices*, the canonical statement of new Keynesian monetary theory, could consider the determinants of inflation with hardly a bank in sight.[6]

In sum, therefore, finance theory and macro-economics together treated financial deepening and increasing leverage as either strongly positive or simply neutral. And that created an environment where the enormous growth in credit as a percentage of GDP raised no particular concerns. And an environment in which, as long as central banks achieved low and stable inflation through appropriate manipulation of the policy interest rate, neither they nor financial regulators needed to have much interest in the aggregate balance sheets of the financial system.

But that turned out to be completely wrong. It might not have turned out wrong if most credit in our economies does what our textbooks say it does. Most undergraduate textbooks of economics, and indeed most advanced academic papers, if they describe what the banking system does, say something like: 'Banks take money from households and lend it to businesses/entrepreneurs, thus allocating credit between alternative capital investment projects.' But as a description of what banks do, or what securitised credit does, in modern advanced economies, that is just wrong.

About 15 % of the credit created by banks and securitised credit markets funds new capital investment by businesses outside the commercial

[6] Woodford (2003).

real estate market. The rest funds either consumption or, essentially, a competition between households or commercial real estate investors for the purchase of assets that already exist—and, in particular, real estate assets. Papers by Òscar Jordá, Moritz Schularick, and Alan Taylor have shown that the phenomenon is not UK-specific: across almost all advanced economies, indeed, the credit system has, over the last half-century, become primarily a system to finance the purchase of real estate.[7] And most of the value of real estate, in turn, lies not in the constructed value of the buildings but, rather, in the locationally specific irreproducible land on which it sits.

That reality, in turn, lies at the core of macroeconomic and financial instability in modern economies. For when credit is extended against existing inelastic supply assets, credit and asset prices become linked in powerful Minsky-type cycles in which more credit drives higher prices, which induces increased credit supply and demand. And the fundamental reason why we have faced such a lengthy post-crisis malaise is that we had, first, an extraordinary strong upswing of the cycle, then a Minsky moment of crisis and confidence loss, and we are now stuck in debt deflation of the sort described by Irving Fisher.[8]

Indeed, I want to stress that debt overhang in the real economy has been a far more important reason for our sustained post-crisis recession than the weakness of the banks on which attention is often focused. The fiscal cost of bank rescue and recapitalisation in 2008 turns out, in retrospect, to have been a very small fraction of the economic harm which the crisis wrought. And over the last five years, the empirical evidence is clear that low demand for credit from over-leveraged real economy companies and households has been a far more important driver of inadequate nominal demand than has a lack of supply of credit from impaired banks.

The total cost across all of the advanced economies of bailing out the banks was certainly considerably less than 3% of GDP: but, on average, the advanced economies are 10% or more below the previous trend. The impact of the credit and asset price cycle is massively more important than insolvency and illiquidity within the financial system itself.

[7] Jordá, Schularick, and Taylor (2014).
[8] Fisher (1933).

So, macroeconomics was completely wrong to suggest that we could ignore aggregate financial system balance sheets and the details of the credit and asset price cycle, as long as inflation stayed low and stable. But what did economics and finance theory say about the second big driver of increasing financial intensity—the rise in intra-financial system complexity?

Here, if anything, it was even clearer that the developments were strongly favourable, treating the complexity of modern finance as clearly beneficial, since it completed more markets and thus brought us closer to the bliss point nirvana of a perfect competitive equilibrium. More trading in more liquid markets delivered improved 'price discovery': derivatives enabled risks to be 'sliced and diced', and distributed into the hands of those best placed to manage them. The Efficient Market Hypothesis proved that financial markets correctly priced future cash flows and allocated capital efficiently. And increasing financial intensity and financial innovation therefore delivered both greater allocative efficiency and greater stability.

Thus, for instance, the IMF's Global Financial Stability Report published in April 2006 reported, with approval, 'the growing recognition that the dispersion of credit risk by banks to a broader and more diverse group of investors has helped make the banking and overall financial system more resilient', and it opined that: 'Improved resilience may be seen in fewer banking failures and more consistent credit provision.' So, we see strong and confident endorsement of increased financial intensity from the bible of financial stability analysis just 15 months before the onset of the biggest financial crisis for 75 years. This was a very strong ideology, an ideology confident that financial markets are inherently efficient and, therefore, that financial deepening and increased complexity is by definition beneficial.

Ideology and Interests

So, how did we get it so wrong? The Queen famously asked the LSE economics faculty why no one saw it coming? The letter sent in reply said that there had been a major collective failure of imagination on behalf of many apparently clever people. So, was this all just a giant intellectual mistake? And where does 'power' come into the picture?

The rising role of the financial system was facilitated by multiple policy changes, starting with the breakdown of Bretton Woods and the liberalisation of domestic credit markets. Those developments were, of course, linked: to maintain a fixed exchange rate system, you have to regulate the domestic credit system; once you move to floating rates, you can at least choose to liberalise the domestic credit system, and in the UK, for instance, the collapse of Bretton Woods was followed very soon thereafter by the somewhat misnamed Competition and Credit Control Act of 1973 which, in fact, largely got rid of previous constraints on credit creation.

The USA saw the gradual dismantling of the McFadden Act limitations on multi-state banking and of the Glass Steagall separation of commercial and investment banking. In the UK in the 1980s, we saw the 'big bang' reforms which removed previous distinctions between brokers and position-takers in the equity market; and we saw increasing freedoms for mutual building societies to move into wider sets of credit market, and to demutualise and become banks. The precise changes reflected the multiple idiosyncrasies of national starting points. But the overall direction of change was common: in multiple countries, we see regulatory change predicated on the assumption that we should treat finance and credit markets as markets like any other, applying the same free-market approaches which have worked well in, say, the market for restaurants or for automobile manufacture. This was a major change from the philosophy which had marked the previous 30 to 40 years of financial repression, during which finance had been treated as a special case requiring more regulation than appropriate in other sectors of the economy.

Why did those deregulations occur? Were they driven by lobbying or were they driven by an ideology? The answer is, of course, a combination. Many were driven by the argument that they were 'inevitable', given what had already occurred; and that argument certainly had some logic. We got rid of fixed exchange rates in part because capital controls were no longer effective in a world of ever-increasing trade flows and foreign direct investment. And once we had got rid of fixed exchange rates, it seemed there was no point in maintaining any capital controls at all. But once you get rid of capital controls, there is no point in trying to control domestic credit, because credit can be provided cross-border. So, at all steps in the process there is an argument which goes: 'Given that finance has been partially liberalised, complete liberalisation is inevitable.'

But liberalisation was also driven by overt lobbying. Thus, for instance, the Japanese banks in the early 1980s, finding that their classic role of providing capital investment credit to major Japanese corporates was being taken over by the global bond markets, argued for the relaxation of the constraints that had previously stopped them being real estate lenders. They then celebrated their lobbying success by unleashing the biggest credit and real estate boom the world had ever seen. And, throughout the negotiations on new bank capital requirements—Basel I and Basel II, the banking industry argued for as loose standards as possible, continually reminding the regulators that, if they were constrained from lending, economic growth would, supposedly, slow.

In some well-documented cases the lobbying was direct, overt, and clearly successful. In the late 1990s, for instance, when Brooksley Born, as chairman of the Commodity Futures Trading Commission (CFTC), argued for regulation of the burgeoning derivatives market, she was countered by huge lobbying from the major banks and investment banks, which were making lots of money out of derivatives. So successful were they that Congress passed a moratorium prohibiting her agency from imposing any new regulations on derivatives.[9] And behind the Gramm–Leach–Bliley Act, which got rid of the Glass–Steagall division between commercial banking and investment banking, we can see the direct influence of well-financed lobbying.

But, alongside lobbying, there were other factors at work. And some aspects of liberalisation were driven by beliefs about its beneficial effect which, while in retrospect quite mistaken, were at the time honestly held. The single-most important driver of the growth of the financial system has been the growth in residential mortgage credit; and rapid growth in mortgage credit was seen as a good thing because, it was said, it would help support wider homeownership.

---

[9] Johnson and Kwak (2011).

That focus on credit to support homeownership can, in turn, however, be seen as a highly imperfect and, in retrospect, dangerous response to rising inequality in political cultures unwilling to consider more fundamental answers. As Raghuram Rajan puts it in his book *Fault Lines* (2011), the American response to rising inequality was, 'Let them eat credit.' There was no agreement on whether it was possible and what actions were required to increase skills, productivity, and relative real wages; and the political culture could not accept increased redistribution. But what everybody could agree on—the bankers, the Democrats and Republicans, the left and the right—was that giving people cheap mortgage credit was a good thing.

So, in relation to the growth of real economy credit and leverage, I think we have to recognise a confluence of private industry interests and apparently desirable social objectives.

As for the belief in complete markets and the efficient-market theory, which seemed to justify the rise in intra-financial system complexity, here, I think we need to recognise that alongside interests, a role was also played by what Robert Skidelsky has labelled 'aesthetics'—the attraction of a complete intellectual system underpinned by elegant mathematics. And here, indeed, we should recognise the power of *language*, of the way in which idea systems can be embedded in words which induce reflex reactions and beliefs so intrinsic that people are unaware of how constrained their thinking has become.

Early in my time at the Financial Services Authority (FSA) in October 2008, I was shown for approval a letter which, jointly authored with the UK Treasury, warned the European Commissioner for Financial Services, Michel Barnier, that he should not introduce what is called a 'skin in the game' retention for distributed credit securities. I told the relevant staff experts that I totally disagreed. We faced a crisis produced by excessive credit creation, partly in the form of securitised credit, which originators had sometimes distributed to investors even when they doubted and disparaged the quality of the underlying credit. A 'skin in the game' retention therefore seemed to me rather a good thing. But the staff experts then warned me that interfering with the 'liquidity' of the credit securities markets would stymie new credit extension to the real economy.

What they did not question was whether more credit extension would actually be a good thing.

The support for more liquidity, more innovation, more credit, had become a reflex so automatic that people could not question the implicit assumptions they were making. And having lived through the crisis at the head of a regulatory authority, I am convinced that these reflexive responses, embedded in language and beliefs, play a crucial role. 'Price discovery' sounds really good because surely we want to 'discover' the truth? 'Efficient markets' sound essential, since who does not love 'efficiency'. 'Market transparency' sounds an undoubted good, because 'transparency' feels like a positive word. 'Market completion' must surely be positive because things are better if 'complete'. But all the words together can combine into a belief system in which it becomes impossible to challenge the idea that more liquidity, more trading, and more financial innovation is always limitlessly better.

Part of the problem, indeed, is that people fall in love with total intellectual systems, systems which appear to provide the answer to all problems. If you know that you are in favour of 'complete markets', then when each new specific problem, each new policy choice, comes along, you have a predefined set of criteria to guide your decision-making. And that means that, while there are also interests at work, they are so intermingled with beliefs that people can hardly recognise their effect.

In regulatory authorities, you often have to employ people who have come from the industry, because only they know what really goes on; only they really know how, for instance, a value-at-risk model works and how you assess risk in derivatives contracts. But they will have internalised the assumption of the industry and, of course, the industry assumes that more liquidity in trading credit securities is good—in part, because they truly believe that and, in part, because they are making a great deal of money out of it.

There is, here, a very subtle self-reinforcing combination of self-interest and ideology which makes it is almost impossible to discern which is the chicken and which the egg. It gets defined in a language that defines which thoughts are sound, which thoughts prove you are part of the orthodoxy, and which statements prove you are outside the orthodoxy and therefore unsound. And, if unsound thoughts are squeezed out, we are less able to see the faults in the orthodoxy before disaster strikes.

References

Andrew, H. (2010). *What is the contribution of the financial sector: Miracle or mirage?*, Chap. 2. The future of banking (LSE Report).

Fisher, I. (1933). The debt-deflation theory of great depressions. *Econometrica, 1*(4), 337–357.

Greenwood, R., & Scharfstein, D. (2013). The growth of finance. *Journal of Economic Perspectives, 27*(2), 3–28.

Johnson, S., & Kwak, J. (2011). *13 Bankers: The Wall Street takeover and the next financial meltdown*. London: Random House.

Jordá, Ò., Schularick, M., & Taylor, A. M. (2014). *The great mortgaging: Housing finance, crises and business cycles* (Working Paper 20501). Cambridge, MA: National Bureau of Economic Research.

Levine, R. (2005). Finance and growth: Theory and evidence. In P. Aghion & S. Durlauf (Eds.), *Handbook of economic growth, 1B*. Netherlands: Elsevier.

Philippon, T., & Reshef, A. (2012). Wages and human capital in the US finance industry: 1909–2006. *Quarterly Journal of Economics, 127*(4), 1551–1609.

Townsend, R. M. (1979). Optimal contracts and competitive markets with costly state verification. *Journal of Economic Theory, 21*(2), 265–293.

Woodford, M. (2003). *Interest and prices: Foundations of a theory of monetary policy*. Princeton, NJ: Princeton University Press.

8

Financialization vs. Efficient Markets: Reframing the Economics and Politics of Finance

Thomas Palley

The Queen's Question and Mainstream Economics

Many readers of this book are probably familiar with the Queen's famous question (5 November 2008) to the faculty of the London School of Economics (LSE) asking why no one foresaw the financial crisis of 2008. The Queen's question has an innocent Hans Anderson 'emperor's new suit' character and it was met with stunned silence. After a few moments of confusion, the distinguished LSE economists responded they needed time to think about it, inadvertently exposing the hollowness of mainstream economics.

In fact, there is a simple and direct answer to the Queen's question, but the distinguished economists could not give it for reasons of professional interest. That answer is, 'We failed to anticipate the crisis because our theory says such things do not happen.' According to mainstream

T. Palley (✉)
Washington, DC, USA

© The Editor(s) (if applicable) and The Author(s) 2016
R. Skidelsky, N. Craig (eds.), *Who Runs the Economy?*,
DOI 10.1057/978-1-137-58017-7_8

economics, the economy is an 'equilibrium system' governed by 'efficient' financial markets. In that system, rational agents anticipate systemic causes of financial crises and prices immediately adjust to prevent them from happening.

This way of thinking has had an enormously profound effect on policy, politics, and society. It has promoted an age of 'market worship' in which financial markets are given special elevated standing. Financial markets are claimed to be the most perfect form of market and they are attributed a special role regarding allocation of capital, promotion of capital accumulation and growth, spreading of risk, and as an instrument of control over managers and corporations.

The financial crisis of 2008, the Great Recession, and the ensuing stagnation have exposed the fallacy of such thinking; they invite a reframing of the politics and economics of finance. This chapter argues that the concept of efficient markets, which has guided thinking about finance and its macroeconomic impacts, should be replaced by the concept of financialisation. The latter refers to the process whereby finance exerts an increasing influence over the real economy, economic policy, and politics. In doing so, it increases income inequality, creates financial fragility and proclivity to economic instability, and generates macroeconomic inefficiency in the form of reduced activity and slower growth.

The Fallacy of the 'Black Swan' and 'Market Failure' Defences

The mainstream economics profession would look silly if it tried to deny the obvious fact that capitalist economies are subject to recurrent financial market turmoil and crises. They have therefore devised two lines of defence: the first is the 'black swan' defence; the second is the 'market failure' defence.

According to black swan theory, problems arise owing to unforeseeable shocks that cannot be anticipated and adjusted for. This defence is the ultimate 'get out of jail free' card, as it invokes a deus ex machina—the black swan. To create a patina of science, so-called swan 'shocks' are dressed up in statistical theory and described as random events drawn from statistical distributions with mathematically defined properties. That description creates a rhetoric that has succeeded in giving credibility to the black swan defence, despite the clear inapplicability and irrelevance of statistical theory to history. Financial crises are part of the historical process, and history is an unrepeatable non-ergodic process. That process is captured by Heraclitus' observation to the effect: 'You cannot step twice in the same river, for other waters are continually flowing.' Statistics applies to repeatable ergodic processes like rolling dice and drawing playing cars: it can never apply to history.

The 'market failure' defence argues financial crises happen because of imperfections in the market mechanism. Within neoclassical economics, this is a very long-standing defence and it is once again being invoked as mainstream economists try to construct new market failures to explain the crisis and stagnation. In mainstream economics, market failures are analogous to epicycles in the Ptolemaic geo-centric model of the cosmos. Every time economists encounter an observation that does not fit they add another market failure—another epicycle.

The problem is that the neoclassical competitive general equilibrium (CGE) model is a Platonic ideal which cannot exist because it does not conform to the real world. It is impossible to transform the real world into the Platonic ideal of CGE theory, which means the market failure defence cannot save the theory as the theory describes an impossible non-existent ideal. Despite this, three generations of economists have mistakenly thought the market failure defence saves their theory. Consequently, the CGE model has been able to retain a tight grip on mainstream economic thinking.

That has had enormous consequences, because economic theory is the prism through which we see and interpret the economy. In a sense, the economy presents a Rorschach test and the prism you hold determines what you see. In Fig. 8.1, if you focus on the sides of the box, you see two faces; if you focus on the top and bottom, you see a vase. When it comes to economics, if you subscribe to CGE theory, you will be inclined towards neoliberal policy recommendations. Abandoning CGE theory and adopting the economic ideas of Keynes (1936) and Minsky (1992) results in fundamentally different perceptions with fundamentally different policy prescriptions.

Fig. 8.1 The power of economic ideas: what you see depends on the ideas you believe

The Triumph of Bad Ideas and the Tragedy of the Past 30 Years

It is understandable why elite moneyed interests are attracted to the prism of neoclassical CGE theory. That theory serves their economic and social interests. The tragedy of the period since the mid-1980s is that labour / social democratic parties have also been captured by this same thinking, albeit tempered with a sprinkling of compassionate policy in the form of more generous welfare payments and more progressive tax systems.

This capture is evident in the fact that the leading academic and policy economists that advise labour and social democratic politicians hold the same core theoretical perspective as advisers to their political opponents. The social democratic advisers only differ in their estimation of the extent and severity of market failures and their assessments of the beneficial capacity of policy to remedy these failures.

The policy consequences have been enormous. In terms of the Rorschach metaphor, it is as though all the major political parties have a common vision of the economy. The political challenge is to compel a change of understanding. In the absence of that, we will remain locked in a neoliberal policy orbit that only fluctuates in the degree of neoliberal intensity.

That raises the issue of 'power'. Mainstream economic ideas are sociologically entrenched and defended by a nexus of inter-locking interests. This reality is particularly clear in the USA with its significantly privatised higher education system. Academic economics is a neoclassical monopoly, organised as a club in which existing club members have an interest in excluding economists of a different theoretical persuasion. The club plays a vital role in educating the chattering class, the business class, the media, and those who will govern. Think-tanks, like the Brookings Institute and the Peterson Institute in Washington DC, extend the monopoly into the realm of public policy and provision of advice to politicians. And academics, think-tanks, and politicians are all supported by the moneyed elites whose interests they promote: the quid pro quo is that the moneyed elite pays academics, think-tanks, and politicians to promote ideas supporting their interests and to block threatening rival ideas.

In his *General Theory*, Keynes (1936, pp. 383–384) wrote about the importance and power of economic ideas, but he was naïve about their source. That source is best understood through Marx's (1845) abiding and penetrating observation in *The German Ideology* that: 'The ideas of the ruling class are in every epoch the ruling ideas, i.e. the class which is the ruling material force of society, is at the same time its ruling intellectual force.'

Mainstream Neoclassical Critiques of Finance

Mainstream economics is dominated by the efficient financial markets hypothesis, but there has always been a fringe critique of that view. Hirshleifer (1971) argued financial markets could lower real output to the extent that they were de facto casinos because operating the casino costs a great deal. Tobin (1984) noted that financial markets actually finance very little investment which, instead, is largely financed by retained profits. He also noted that many financial market activities may be unproductive so that bankers, brokers, and traders are paid far more than they contribute to economic production. Willem Buiter, with his customary stinging wit, argues that derivatives market traders are actually irrational:

'I have yet to meet a trader who did not believe that he or she could not beat the market. Because these traders effectively are the market, they are collectively irrational, as they cannot beat themselves.'[1]

This financial markets critique from the mainstream fringe is welcome. However, it remains an 'insider' critique trapped in the efficient-market discourse which is framed by the neoclassical ideal of a perfect economy. Inefficiency is the result of departure from this ideal. Consequently, mainstream critiques of finance do not surface more profound issues regarding the power of finance and its broader negative macroeconomic impacts. In terms of the Rorschach metaphor, insider critiques of the efficient-market hypothesis remain blind to other interpretations of the economy. That limitation points to the significance of the theory of financialisation, which provides a critique of finance based on a different vision of the economy. In doing so, it generates a significantly different policy reform agenda.

The Macroeconomics of Financialisation

Financialisation refers to the increased presence and power of finance within the economy, resulting in 'the domination of the macro economy and economic policy by financial interests' (Palley, 2013, p. 1). Empirically, financialisation increases the significance of the financial sector relative to the real sector; transfers income from the real sector to the financial sector, increasing the financial sector's share of GDP; and contributes to wage stagnation and increased income inequality.

Financialisation raises concerns with power, stability, and macroeconomic efficiency. The concern with power relates to finance's ability to restructure the economy and redistribute income to owners of financial capital. The concern with macroeconomic stability relates to finance's capacity to destabilise economies, as evidenced in the US economy by the stock market crash of 1987, the Long Term Capital Management crisis of 1998, the stock market technology bubble of the late 1990s and 2000, the housing bubble of the 2000s, and the financial crisis of 2008. The concern with macroeconomic efficiency concerns the adverse impact on economic activity and growth.

---

[1] Buiter (2009).

Finance's power to restructure is illustrated by the history since 1980. Until the late 1970s, developed country economies could be described as a Keynesian virtuous circle growth model in which wages were the engine of demand growth. This model is illustrated in Fig. 8.2 and the economic logic was as follows. Productivity growth drove wage growth which fuelled demand growth. That promoted full employment which provided the incentive to invest, which drove further productivity growth.

Within this virtuous circle framework, finance was characterised by a public utility model based on New Deal regulation. Its role was to provide business and entrepreneurs with finance for investment, to provide business and households with insurance services, and to provide households with means of saving for future needs.

After 1980, the virtuous circle Keynesian growth model was replaced by a neoliberal growth model. The two key changes were the abandonment of the policy commitment to full employment, which was replaced by a commitment to stable low inflation, and the severing of the link between wages and productivity growth. These changes created a new economic model. Before 1980, wages were the engine of demand growth; after 1980, debt and asset price inflation became the engines of demand growth.

As illustrated in Fig. 8.3, the new economic model can be described as a 'neoliberal policy box' that fences workers in and pressures them from all sides via:

- a corporate model of globalisation;
- the small government agenda that attacks public sector activity;

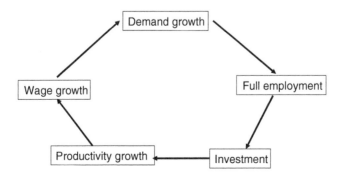

Fig. 8.2   The 1945–1980 virtuous circle Keynesian growth model

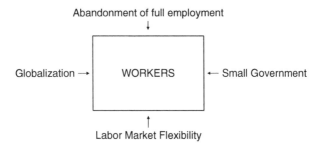

Fig. 8.3   The neoliberal policy box

- the so-called labour market flexibility agenda that attacks unions and worker protections; and
- the replacement of full employment policy with low inflation targeting policy.

With regard to the financial system, the New Deal public utility model was slowly gutted by deregulation and subsequent financial innovations were left largely unregulated (Palley, 2012, ch. 5).

The combination of the neoliberal box model and the gutting of the public utility model of finance created a new system characterised by wage stagnation, increasing income inequality and growing financial instability. The macroeconomic workings of this economy are illustrated in Fig. 8.4. Within the real economy, the configuration of economic policies embodied in the neoliberal policy box generated wage stagnation and increased inequality, which contributed to creation of a structural demand shortage. Within the financial economy, financial innovation, deregulation, speculation, and fraud combined to produce a long-running 30-year credit bubble that fuelled borrowing and asset price inflation, which papered over the demand shortage problem. This bubble process was accommodated by easy monetary policy that sequentially lowered interest rates every time the bubble threatened to burst.

This economic configuration was sustained until the financial crisis of 2008, albeit the business cycle weakened in the 2000s despite an intensified asset bubble. However, the process came to an abrupt halt with the bursting of the credit bubble in 2008. With interest rates near zero and economic agents heavily indebted, monetary policy has been unable to

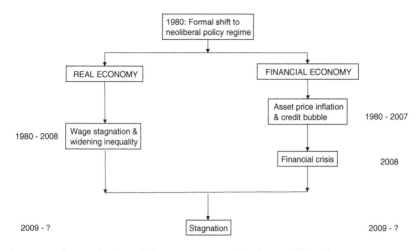

Fig. 8.4 The evolution of the US economy in the Neoliberal Era, 1980–2015

Table 8.1 Average income share of bottom 90 % of households

	1951–1960	1961–1970	1971–1980	1981–1990	1991–2000	2001–2007	*2007*	2008–2012	2012
Bottom 90 % share (including capital gains)	66.5	66.0	66.4	62.0	58.8	53.3	*50.3*	51.8	49.6
Bottom 90 % share (excluding capital gains)	68.1	68.2	67.7	64.5	59.1	55.9	*54.3*	53.5	51.9

Source: Author's calculations using data from Piketty & Saez, Tables A1 and A3, http://elsa.Berkeley.edu/~saez/TabFig2013prel.xls

jump-start the credit expansion process as in the three previous downturns (1982, 1991, and 2001). Without the credit bubble to fill the structural demand gap created by the neoliberal policy box, the USA has suffered from demand shortage and stagnation.

Evidence supporting this story is clearly visible in data for the US economy. Table 8.1 shows the average income share of the bottom 90 % of US households according to the Piketty and Saez database, which uses tax return information. The table shows that the share of total income of the bottom 90 % was stable at approximately 66 % from 1950 to

Table 8.2 Average income share of top 1 % of households

	1951–1960	1961–1970	1971–1980	1981–1990	1991–2000	2001–2007	*2007*	2008–2012	2012
Top 1 % share (including capital gains)	10.6	10.3	9.3	13.0	16.7	20.1	*23.5*	20.2	22.5
Top 1 % share (excluding capital gains)	9.2	8.2	7.9	10.2	14.1	16.6	*18.3*	17.8	19.3

Source: Author's calculations using data from Piketty & Saez, Tables A1 and A3, http://elsa.Berkeley.edu/~saez/TabFig2013prel.xls

1980. Thereafter, it began a rapid decline, falling to 50.3 % in 2007, one year before the financial crisis. After briefly recovering during the Great Recession (2008–2009) as profits and the income of the top 10 % declined, the income share of the bottom 90 % has resumed its decline in the ensuing weak recovery. This finding holds regardless of whether income is measured with or without capital gains.[2]

Table 8.2 shows the average income share of the top 1 % of US households, which is again derived from the Piketty and Saez database. The table tells the other side of the story contained in Table 8.1 and shows that higher-income households have seen an increase in their income share. The important feature in Table 8.2 is that the top 1 % of income earners have gained disproportionately, so that income redistribution has been concentrated at the top. That matters because higher-income households have a higher propensity to save.[3] Consequently, redistributing income to the top increases aggregate saving and weakens aggregate demand, which contributes to explaining stagnation in the wake of the Great Recession.

Table 8.3 shows the distribution of income gains in each business cycle expansion since World War II. In the expansions from 1949 through to

---

[2] If capital gains income is excluded, the share of the bottom 90 % is slightly larger as capital gains flow disproportionately to the top 10 % of households who are wealthier and own more property, real and financial.

[3] Carroll (2000).

Table 8.3 Distribution of income growth by business cycle expansion across the wealthiest top 10 % and bottom 90 % of households

	1949–1953	1954–1957	1959–1960	1961–1969	1970–1973	1975–1979	1982–1990	1991–2000	2001–2007	2009–2012	Average Pre-1908	Average Post-1980
Top 10 % of households	20 %	28	32	33	43	45	80	73	98	116	34 %	92 %
Bottom 90 % of households	80 %	72	68	67	57	55	20	27	2	–16	66 %	8 %

Source: Tcherneva (2014), published in The New York Times, September 26, 2014

Table 8.4 Selected indicators of the growth of the financial sector relative to the overall economy

	FIRE output/GDP (%)	Financial/Non-financial profits (%)
1973	13.6	20.1
1979	14.4	19.7
1989	17.9	26.2
2000	20.1	39.3
2007	20.4	44.6

Note: FIRE = finance, insurance, and real estate.
Source: Palley (2013), Tables 2.6, 2.7, and 2.11

Table 8.5 Debt-to-GDP ratio and growth rate

	1950	1980	2007
Domestic non-financial sector debt–GDP ratio	1.34	1.38	2.20
Domestic financial sector debt–GDP ratio	0.03	0.20	1.12
Domestic non-financial + financial sector debt–GDP ratio	1.37	1.58	3.32
	1950–1979	**1980–2007**	
Average annual growth of real GDP (%)	4.0 %	3.0	

Source: Bureau of Economic Analysis, Federal Reserve Board (Financial Accounts of the USA) and author's calculations

1979, the bottom 90 % of households always received more than half the gains, albeit the trend was downward. After 1980, there is an abrupt and extreme change, and the share of income gains going to the bottom 90 % plummets. In the most recent expansion, which began in 2010, the bottom 90 % has had negative gains. Rather than sharing in the growth of aggregate income, the bottom 90 % has suffered a decline in income: conversely, the top 10 % have gained more than the increase in total income.

Tables 8.4 and 8.5 describe developments in the financial economy that accompanied these developments in the real economy. Table 8.4 shows the enormous increase in the size of the financial sector relative to the real sector, and the increase in financial sector profits relative to the profits of the real sector. In the 30 years preceding the financial crisis, the financial sector has increased its share of US gross domestic product (GDP), reaching more than 20 % in 2007. Over that period, its profits relative to non-financial sector profits more than doubled.

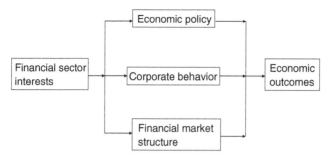

Fig. 8.5   Main conduits of financialization

Table 8.5 shows a dramatic increase in the debt-to-GDP ratio after the inauguration of the neoliberal era. In the 30 years from 1950 to 1980, the debt to-GDP ratio rose fractionally from 1.37 to 1.58, and the domestic non-financial sector's debt-to-GDP ratio was essentially constant. After 1980, there is a dramatic increase in debt-to-GDP ratio of both the domestic non-financial sector and the financial sector. In the 27 years from 1980 to 2007, the aggregate debt-to-GDP ratio rises from 1.58 to 3.32. However, the average annual real GDP growth rate falls from 4% to 3%, so that the era of financialisation is actually associated with slower growth. That is consistent with the cross-country study findings of Cecchetti and Kharroubi, from the Bank of International Settlements, who report that too large a financial sector lowers growth.[4]

The Microeconomics and Political Economy of Financialisation

Finance has played an essential role in creating and maintaining the new economic model. That role is illustrated in Fig. 8.5, which shows how the impact of finance has operated through three conduits. First, finance used its political power, derived from money, to promote the economic policies on which the new model rests. Thus, finance lobbied for financial

---

[4] Cecchetti and Kharroubi (2012).

deregulation; supported the shift of macroeconomic policy away from focusing on full employment to focusing on inflation; supported corporate globalisation and expanding international mobility of real and financial capital; supported privatisation, diminished regulation and a more regressive tax code; and supported the attack on unions and employment protections, with the aim of lowering wages and strengthening the hand of management.

Second, finance took control of business and compelled it to adopt financial sector behaviours and perspectives. The change was justified by appealing to economists' notion of shareholder value maximisation. The result of this change in corporate behaviour was adoption of the leverage buyout model that loaded firms with debt, the adoption of a short-term business perspective that undermined willingness to undertake long-term investment projects, the adoption of impossibly high required rates of return that also undercut long-term investment, support for offshoring of production to take advantage of lower labour costs, and the adoption of Wall Street-styled pay packages for top management and directors.

Third, the combination of deregulated financial markets and financial innovation provided the supply of credit needed to finance leveraged buy-outs, takeovers, and stock buybacks. The increased supply of credit also supported consumer borrowing and mortgage borrowing that inflated house prices, thereby filling the 'demand shortage' created by wage stagnation, trade deficits, and investment offshoring.

Putting Finance Back in the Box

The overarching task is to restore shared prosperity, which requires rebuilding the wage-productivity growth link and having economic policy commit to full employment. That task is twofold. First, it is to remake the rules and policies governing the real economy so that workers share in the fruits of economic growth. Second, it is to rein in the financial sector, which has been a principal driver of so much adverse change in the real economy.

This task can be understood through the lens of economic institutionalism. The American institutionalist economist John R. Commons

(1862–1945) made the 'transaction' the centre of his economic theory. The role of institutions (which includes regulation and policy) is to impose some degree of collective control over transactions so that they deliver socially desired outcomes. Financialisation involves finance using its powers to structure the economy's transactions to its advantage. Putting finance back in the box involves designing a different set of institutions that deliver other socially preferred economic outcomes.

With regard to the task of restructuring the real economy, the details of the needed policy programme are beyond the scope of this chapter. However, the programme is briefly summarised in Fig. 8.6. Politically, the challenge is to overthrow the neoliberal paradigm and replace it with a 'structural Keynesian' paradigm that 'repacks' the policy box, taking workers out and putting corporations and financial markets in. The goal is to have corporations and financial markets serve a broader public interest instead of shareholder value maximisation. That requires replacing corporate globalisation with managed globalisation which incorporates labour and environmental standards and prohibitions on currency manipulation; restoring macroeconomic policy commitment to full employment; replacing the neoliberal anti-government agenda with a social democratic government agenda that ensures investment in infrastructure, health, and education; and replacing the neoliberal labour market flexibility with a solidarity-based labour market policies that rebuilds worker bargaining power via increased trade union membership, a robust minimum wage, and efficient worker protections.

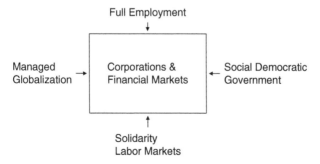

Fig. 8.6 The structural Keynesian box

The second task is reforming financial markets and corporate governance so that they help the real economy deliver shared prosperity. One challenge is political and concerns electoral and campaign finance reform. The political power of finance rests on money, which is why it is so critical to reduce the role of money in politics. In the absence of campaign finance reform, finance and corporate interests will retain the power to distort the democratic process and block necessary economic policy reform.

A second challenge is changing corporate behaviour. This requires reform of corporate governance that makes business more accountable, changes the incentives that promote current business practice, and recognises the interests of stakeholders other than shareholders.

A third challenge is to regain control over financial markets. Figure 8.7 illustrates a four-part programme for putting financial markets back in the box so that they promote shared and more sustainable forms of prosperity. The top edge of the box indicates the need for monetary policy to re-commit to full employment, which requires abandoning rigid ultra-low inflation targeting and recognising that monetary policy can permanently influence the level of economic activity. The left edge of the box concerns the need for tough regulations that impose appropriate capital and liquidity requirements on financial institutions, and also the barring of banks from engaging in speculative activity using government insured deposits—the so-called Volker rule. Of course, regulation also must be

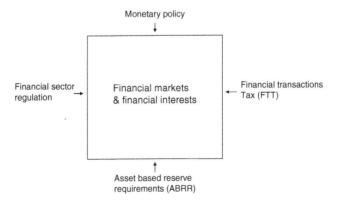

Fig. 8.7 Putting finance back in the box

also enforced, which speaks to the importance of a good government agenda that ensures the integrity, financing, and operational efficiency of regulatory agencies.

The right edge of the box concerns the need for a financial transactions tax (FTT). An FTT can raise revenue, help shrink the financial sector to more appropriate and healthy proportions, and discourage damaging speculative transactions (Palley, 2001).

Lastly, the bottom edge of the box advocates that the Federal Reserve institute a system of asset-based reserve requirements (ABRR) that covers the entire financial sector (Palley, 2003, 2009). ABRR require financial firms to hold reserves against different classes of assets, and the regulatory authority sets adjustable reserve requirements on the basis of its concerns with each asset class. By adjusting the reserve requirement on each asset class, the central bank can change the return on that asset class, thereby affecting incentives to invest in the asset class.

The US house price bubble showed that central banks cannot manage the economy with just interest rate policy targeted on inflation and unemployment. Doing that leaves the economy exposed to financial excess. Interest rate policy must therefore be supplemented by balance sheet controls, which is the role of ABRR.

ABRR provide a new set of policy instruments that can address specific financial market excess by targeting specific asset classes, leaving interest rate policy free to manage the overall macroeconomic situation. ABRR are especially useful for preventing asset price bubbles, as reserve requirements can be increased on over-heated asset categories. For instance, a house price bubble can be surgically targeted by increasing reserve requirements on new mortgages. That makes new mortgages more expensive without raising interest rates and damaging the rest of the economy.

Finally, ABRR can be used to promote socially desirable investments and 'green' investments that are needed to address climate change. Loans for such investment projects can be given a negative reserve requirement that can be credited against other reserve requirements, thereby encouraging banks to finance those projects in order to earn the credit. In sum, ABRR provide a comprehensive framework for collaring the financial sector and ensuring it promotes shared prosperity.

Conclusion: Beyond Orthodox Economics

We live in an age of market worship. Orthodox economics fuels that worship; and it also gives special standing to financial markets, which are represented as the most perfect form of market. Of course, there is also some critique of the functional efficiency and casino aspects of financial markets, but these critiques stop far short of the financialisation critique. Consequently, orthodox diagnoses of the financial crisis and policy recommendations stop far short of what is needed to put finance back in the box.

The economic evidence clearly shows the need to make finance serve the real economy, rather than having the real economy serve finance, as is now the case. It can be done. The challenge is to get a hearing for policies that will do so. Meeting that challenge requires getting new economic ideas on the table, which is why the debate about economics and the economy is so important. However, the road to policy change runs through politics. Putting finance back in the box therefore also requires breaking the political power of finance, which is why campaign finance reform, electoral reform, and popular political engagement are equally important.

References

Buiter, W. (2009, 12 April). Useless finance, harmful finance and useful finance. *Financial Times*.

Carroll, C. D. (2000). Why do the rich save so much? In J. Slemrod (Ed.), *Does Atlas shrug? The economic consequences of taxing the rich*. Russell Sage Foundation at Harvard University Press.

Cechetti, S. G., & Kharroubi, E. (2012). *Reassessing the impact of finance on growth* (BIS Working Paper No. 381). Basel, Switzerland: Bank of International Settlements.

Hirshleifer, J. (1971). The private and social value of information and the reward to inventive activity. *American Economics Review, 61*, 561–574.

Keynes, J. M. (1936). *The general theory of employment, interest, and money*. London: Macmillan.

Minsky, H. P. (1992 [1993]). The financial instability hypothesis (Working paper No. 74). New York: The Jerome Levy Economics Institute of Bard

College (published in Arestis, P., & Sawyer, M. (Eds.), *Handbook of radical political economy*. Aldershot: Edward Elgar).

Palley, T. I. (2001). Destabilizing speculation and the case for an international currency transactions tax. *Challenge, 44*(May/June), 70–89.

Palley, T. I. (2003). Asset price bubbles and the case for asset-based reserve requirements. *Challenge, 46*(May/June), 53–72.

Palley, T. I. (2009). A better way to regulate financial markets: Asset based reserve requirements. Amherst: Economists' Committee for Safer, Accountable, Fair and Efficient Financial Reform, University of Massachusetts. Available at http://www.peri.umass.edu/fileadmin/pdf/other_publication_types/SAFERbriefs/SAFER_issue_brief15.pdf

Palley, T. I. (2012). *From financial crisis to stagnation: The destruction of shared prosperity and the role of economics*. Cambridge: Cambridge University Press.

Palley, T. I. (2013). *Financialization: The macroeconomics of finance capital domination*. New York: Macmillan/Palgrave.

Tcherneva, P. R. (2014). Reorienting fiscal policy: A bottom-up approach. *Journal of Post Keynesian Economics, 37*(1), 43–66.

Tobin, J. (1984). On the efficiency of the financial system. *Lloyds Bank Review, 153*, 1–15.

9

Power and Inequality

James K. Galbraith and Anthony Heath

Power and Inequality by James K. Galbraith

As an economist, my pursuits are prosaic. I deal not with grand ideas but with grubby details. Among my vices, the Ricardian does not number. I consider that sensible policies grow only from useful local knowledge, and that useful local knowledge relies, in part though not in whole, on meticulous and well-considered measurement. My ideal economist was described by Keynes in his sketch of Marshall: 'purposeful and disinterested in a simultaneous mood; as aloof and incorruptible as an artist, yet sometimes as near the earth as a politician'[1]

In that spirit, my main line of research for 20 years has addressed a seemingly simple problem: measurements of economic inequality at the national

---

[1] Keynes (1933).

J.K. Galbraith (✉)
University of Texas, Austin, TX, USA

A. Heath
Centre for Social Investigation, Nuffield College, Oxford

© The Editor(s) (if applicable) and The Author(s) 2016
R. Skidelsky, N. Craig (eds.), *Who Runs the Economy?*,
DOI 10.1057/978-1-137-58017-7_9

level. These have long been inadequate for realistic comparison across countries or through time. The main reason lies in a heavy reliance on surveys. Surveys are expensive; they are taken sporadically, and especially so in the poorer lands; and the survey designs and target concepts (income, expenditure, gross or net of tax, households or persons as the reporting unit, household-size adjustments) vary from time to time and place to place. The result is a cacophony of measurements, except in a small number of the wealthiest countries. Econometricians have attempted to compensate for the noise with sophisticated statistics; the effort has not worked.

A recent fashionable alternative has been the use of income tax data, especially to measure the income shares of the topmost strata. But income tax data are available only in those countries that have income tax. In a recent iteration of the Top Incomes data set, these numbered 29; most of them either of Anglo-Saxon heritage or in continental Europe.[2] Moreover, taxable income for income tax purposes is defined by tax law and this differs across countries and varies through time. In the USA, the Tax Reform Act of 1986 expanded the definition of taxable income while covering the spectrum of that income for the wealthiest taxpayers at a lower marginal rate. This revenue-neutral, broadly progressive reform now turns up on the statistical radar screen as a dramatic increase in the top share of incomes. Apart from the legal redefinition of income, nothing occurred in 1986 or 1987 that would have produced any such thing.

The philosopher Charles Sanders Peirce wrote of Kepler that he:

> undertook to draw a curve through the places of Mars, and his greatest service to science was in impressing on men's minds that this was the thing to be done if they wished to improve astronomy; that they were not to content themselves with inquiring whether one system of epicycles was better than another, but that they were to sit down to the figures and find out what the curve, in truth was.

This has been my credo for many years, and the question has been, how to apply it in this particular domain?

My answer derives from expedience and also from fractal geometry and elementary information theory.

---

[2] Facundo Alvaredo, Anthony B. Atkinson, Thomas Piketty, and Emmanuel Saez, *The World Top Incomes Database*, http://topincomes.parisschoolofeconomics.eu/

Expedience suggested that if better measures were ever to be found, intermittent ad hoc surveys of random samples of households would not do. The effort would have to rely on data sets collected consistently, over long periods of time, for ulterior purposes, with wide coverage, by stable authorities.

Fractal geometry suggested that random sampling might not be necessary. A selective (or 'biased') sub-sample of an economy—such as the manufacturing sector—might be sufficient to indicate the general behaviour of distribution—just as one can peer through a window and tell the weather, without taking a random sample of pixels from the sky.

Information theory taught me that a generalised entropy measure of information could be transformed into an inequality statistic—the Theil statistic—with the attractive property that measures taken at the group level (using only group average income and group size) would often be consistent in their behaviour with measures that might have been taken at the individual level, but were not.

So, it stood to reason that one might be able to measure comparative levels and the evolution of economic inequalities from administrative data sets, collected for tax, trade, industrial planning, or other purposes over long periods by bureaucratic routine, and published as tables semi-aggregated by some classification scheme, usually either industrial, sectoral, or geographic, and sometimes a blend of two of these types, such as sectors within regions. It remained to test this proposition and we found that it was easy to do so, especially using data for the manufacturing sectors which are compiled by most governments with reasonable consistency over long intervals. Given clean source data, a global inequality data set with thousands of observations can be generated on a spread sheet overnight.

For many purposes, a measure of pay inequality across industrial sectors is the appropriate tool—for instance, if one is interested in the effect on relative wage rates of technology or trade, or of macroeconomic developments such as changing unemployment or exchange rates, or of international forces such as global interest rates and the oil price. Similarly, with regional or sectoral data one can develop an informative portrait of changing relative position within countries, as we have done for Russia, China, India, the European Union, several large Latin American countries, and the USA. In the US case, we have shown how to string together different data sources to produce inequality measurements back to 1920.

Still, for many audiences the between-groups component of a Theil T-statistic is not an intuitive measure. And it is difficult to compare directly with the Gini coefficients of household income inequalities with which many researchers in economics and the larger public are most familiar, and which form the main available comparators for our measures. For this reason, we sought to discover whether there was a stable correspondence between a T-statistic measured across the manufacturing sector in a standardised international data set—namely, the Industrial Statistics of the United Nations Industrial Development Organization—and a selection of survey-based Gini coefficients.

We learned that, after controlling for the income/expenditure concept and several other characteristics of the survey-based measures, the Theil measure is more volatile but otherwise the correspondence is very close, over more than 400 overlapping country-year observations.

This finding permitted us to generate a data set of estimated measures of household gross income inequality, called Estimated Household Income Inequality (EHII), in Gini coefficient format, with over 3800 observations for 149 countries during the period from 1963 to 2008. This is the largest consistent cross-national data set of income inequalities in existence that does not rely on interpolations over missing years or across missing countries. It is available on the website of the University of Texas Inequality Project at http://utip.gov.utexas. edu, along with working papers and other materials explaining the calculations and interpreting the results. An update to 2010 or 2011 is under way.

A recent undertaking has been to evaluate the quality of the EHII estimates against other measures. These are of two broad types: the individual survey-based estimates that are calculated and published by government agencies, private research enterprises, and individual academics for particular countries and years; and the large transnational data sets that have appeared in recent times, published by the World Bank, the OECD, the European Union, the Economic Commission for Latin America and the Luxembourg Income Studies.

We found that the EHII measures are highly compatible with the measurements produced, mainly for the wealthy countries, by the Luxembourg Income Study (LIS), the OECD and the EU; moreover,

EHII has far more observations than any of these alternatives.[3] There are cases, however—especially among large developing countries, including Brazil and South Africa—where the EHII measures fall below those taken in surveys. The reasons for this remain unclear, beyond the fact that such countries have both wealth and poverty on atypical scales. In the USA, EHII does not capture the rise in taxable incomes reported at the top of the income scale after 1990; this is not surprising since that rise is known to originate in the financial and capital markets, and not so much in increasing inequality of wages. In comparison to EHII, the World Development Indicators of the World Bank stands out as an example of a sparse, inconsistent, and unreliable agglomeration of measures; yet, apart from EHII, it is the only data set based on independent calculations for each observation that has been presented as having global scope and measures that are presented as being directly comparable across countries and over time.[4]

What, then, can one learn from examining a substantial panel data set of inequality measures spanning a half-century? An immediate consequence is renewed respect for the American economist of Belorussian origin, Simon Kuznets, born in Pinsk in 1901. In 1955, Kuznets argued for a simple model of pay inequalities, determined mainly by the average differential between industry and agriculture, and by the relative size of these two major sectors.[5] In general, he argued, as development matures, an emerging middle class reduces overall inequality in the richer countries. This model can be adapted in numerous useful ways to the more diversified and differentiated global economy that exists today, but the underlying principle remains. It is that inter-sectoral transitions and changing average incomes across groups as overall income increases remain the prime determinants of changing inequality.

---

[3] Galbraith, Choi, Halbach, Malinowska, and Zhang (2015).

[4] The World Income Inequality Data (WIID) set of the United Nations University World Institute for Development Economics Research is a valuable bibliographic collection, but the data need to be sorted in various ways before the values in them can be treated as comparative measures. The valuable Standardized World Income Inequality Data set (SWIID) of the University of Iowa is a synthetic data set drawn, in part, from the EHII, and heavily reliant on interpolation across time and countries.

[5] Kuznets (1955).

In Kuznets' version, where an agricultural economy of freeholders (or communes, as in China) provides an egalitarian starting point, then inequality first rises under industrialisation and then falls—the famous inverted 'U'. But if the starting point is a slave economy, a serf economy, or a dual economy of subsistence farming and resource extraction, then the Kuznets income-inequality surface may be predominantly downward sloping over its entire range. And that is what the data reveal.

Presently the richest countries of the world, specifically the social democracies of Northern Europe, have the lowest inequalities. The countries with high income inequalities are those in the developing world, and especially in the tropics: Latin America, Africa, and South and Southeast Asia. Two significant exceptions are the communist lands, which, in their day, had low inequality for their income level, and some of the richest countries in the era of globalisation, such as the USA and the UK, which have high inequality due the high share of income derived from the capital markets. China is a rare example in the modern world of the classical Kuznets case: rising inequality along with income in the early stages of industrialisation. But even in China the peak of the Kuznets inverted-U seems recently to have been reached.[6]

A second finding concerns trends. These are continental and global, not national. They bear a distinct relationship to financial regimes. After 1971, with the dissolution of the stabilising Bretton Woods framework, there was a global commodities and credit boom, and in many developing countries inequalities declined, although in some of the advanced countries, whose terms of trade were hurt, inequalities increased. After 1980, with the arrival of high interest rates and debt crises, there was a worldwide movement towards massively higher inequality, first in the developing world, then in the breakdown of the communist system, and finally in Asia. One may say that the pressure for rising inequality was effective in inverse proportion to the strength of institutional structures that resisted it.

A finding of common global forces and particular movements through time enables us to dispense with convenient myths about technology, education, and skill. I first demolished the hypothesis of 'skill-biased

6 Zhang (2014).

technological change' as a driver of inequality in a book published in 1998.[7] Many others have followed but, for serious students of inequality, the skills hypothesis lost interest years ago.

The rise of global inequality peaked provisionally in 2000, with the crash that ended the information technology boom in the USA, and then the change in the world financial climate following the events of September 11, 2001. Interest rates on secure short-term assets fell sharply. There followed a general revival of commodity markets and industrial development throughout the world, and inequality—though still high by historical standards—began again to decline. We have documented this decline in wage data for parts of Latin America, for China, for parts of Europe, and for Russia and other post-Soviet states. Whether we have entered a new 'era of declining inequality', time will tell.

In a recent book, Professor Thomas Piketty of the Paris School of Economics has argued that rising inequality is inexorable under capitalism, due to a tendency for the rate of return on financial capital to exceed the rate of growth of income.[8] Without getting into the particulars of that argument, the evidence described above suggests a different general rule. Rising inequality is the artefact of particular moments in the history of financial capitalism, when strong pressures at the continental or global levels overwhelm the institutional defences that societies seek to erect, whose purpose is to provide stabilising protections against the ravages of extreme inequality.

The neoliberal era was such a period; it began in the late 1970s and continued until the end of the century. The neoliberal era was a period of savagely rising inequalities within most countries, mitigated at the world level only by the rapidly rising average real income in one formerly poor but never neoliberal country, China. The tocsin of the era sounded in 1997 with the Asian crisis, in 1998 with the Russian devaluation, and again in 2002 with the Argentine default and subsequent rapid recovery. Since that time, alternative models have been developing throughout the world. Even in the heartland of neoliberal ideology, the USA, the ideo-

---

[7] Galbraith (1998).
[8] Piketty (2013).

logical onslaught of inequality-increasing measures has waned. And so, too, has the rise in economic inequalities.

Therefore, in contrast to Professor Piketty, I maintain that economic inequality is a contingent condition, subject in principle to effective regulation and to control.

More generally, the role that effective regulation plays in economic life has been widely misunderstood. The neoliberal view holds that regulation imposes burdens as well as benefits, and therefore may be imposed or dispensed with according to whether one is greater, or less, than the other. This view embodies a deep and drastic misunderstanding. For, as any engineer knows, without regulation machines overheat. As any biologist knows, without regulation organisms die.

In economics, the boundaries imposed by regulation are indispensable. Airlines do not fly without air traffic control, drugs require testing, meat and milk must be inspected, banks left unsupervised fall prey to crooks.[9] Indeed, the principal difference between 'developed' and 'less-developed' societies is not 'human capital' or access to specific technology. It is the functioning of reasonable and efficient laws and regulations, and the willingness of the population to live by and to respect them. The control of economic inequalities, and therefore of predatory behaviour, especially by oligarchs, is an instance of this requirement for successful civilisation and sustainable economics.

The principal challenge facing national economies is therefore to design, build, and maintain an effective, autonomous, fair, competent, and efficient regulatory service, and to do so in the face of instabilities and disruptions from within and from without. Financial regulation is an element of this challenge with obvious implications for inequality. So, too, are minimum wages, labour rights, and effective taxation of income, profits, and land value. So, too, of course, is the ultimate challenge of controlling and coping with climate change.

In large countries, including the USA, Russia, and China, as well as Brazil, effective regulation can be pursued at the national level. In regions composed of smaller units—even in Europe, where some of the units are very large—international experiments have been tried. These deserve a word.

---

[9] The criminal element in the Great Financial Crisis is well-documented, as are the recent multiple depredations of HSBC.

The tragedy of modern Europe is that the design of its transnational economic system occurred under the shadow of Mrs Thatcher. It therefore embodies the delusions of market self-regulation that were common to her time. The result has been an ongoing disaster in Southern Europe, against which the peoples of those countries—in the first instance, the Greeks—are now rising up. The new Greek government has the forces of reason and history on its side. But where (as in Europe) the neoliberal ethos aligns with national and not merely with corporate interests, and where inequalities are especially pronounced across national borders rather than only within them, then power relations are especially strong and the prospect for an effective reconstruction along sustainable lines is bleak.

I have observed, from time to time, that large political entities do not long survive the departure of even their smallest members. The Soviet Union did not survive the departure of the Baltic states. Yugoslavia did not survive the departure of Slovenia. The USA in 1860 did not survive the departure of South Carolina—said at the time to be 'too small for a republic, too large for an insane asylum'. It took a long war to restore the previous Union.

Europe most urgently requires an ethic of trans-European solidarity and mutual assistance. It needs, and lacks, a means of supporting the incomes of its most vulnerable households, wherever they may be, and without going through local or national governments that may be ineffective, corrupt, or merely bankrupt. Europe needs a common programme for investment, debt relief, and financial reform—all measures that would reduce trans-European inequalities.[10] In these respects, the European problem is an instance of the larger questions to which this chapter has been addressed.

---

[10] See Yanis Varoufakis, Stuart Holland, and James K. Galbraith, *The Modest Proposal*, http://yanis-varoufakis.eu/euro-crisis/modest-proposal/

Power and Inequality by Anthony Heath

Conventional economic analysis is built on individualistic micro foundations, and this applies as much to discussions and measurements of inequality as it does in other areas of economics. However, a great deal of political science and sociological literature is focused on the relationships between social groups, not simply between individuals. For example, C. Wright Mills' classic study *The Power Elite* (1956) was talking not about individuals having power, but about a group of inter-connected elites. For Mills, the interconnections between the industrial, the military, and the political elites was central. Many other treatments of political power also focus on relationships between groups. Marx, for example, also focused on the key role of organised groups. Economists, and many social scientists, are much happier with the idea of categories, but what was important in both Mills and, before that, Marx is this idea of organised groups with distinctive material interests but also with their distinctive patterns of ties, social interconnections, and subjective awareness of their shared interests. This is what is missing from a great deal of economics: it is this idea that individuals influence each other and do not behave solely as atomised individuals.

There is a mismatch, then, between the standard political-science approach to the study of power, which is much more concerned with the power which more or less organised groups possess, and the individualistic models of standard economic theory which typically ignore processes of social influence and organisation. To be sure, it would be a travesty to say that all economists take this view. The Nobel prize-winner George Akerlof, in particular, has been notable for drawing on psychological and sociological theory and research to incorporate social influence and group processes into economic theory. Akerlof and Kranton (2002), for example, draw on the sociological literature to develop group-based explanations in the economics of education. But most mainstream economics, including much of the work on inequality, remains essentially individualistic.

One response to this mismatch has been to construct metrics for measuring political power analogous to economic measures of income or wealth inequality, using an individualistic approach (see, for example,

Gelman, Katz, & Tuerlinckx, 2002). These measures, first invented by the mathematician Lionel Penrose in 1946, are of considerable interest in their own right and are not uninformative about power inequalities in electoral systems. In essence, one constructs a *power* index defined by the *probability* of an individual's vote changing the *outcome* of an election. So, for example, a swing voter in a marginal constituency is going to have considerably greater voting power than a voter in a safe seat. These power indices have been used for investigating, for example, the distribution of voting power among EU member states in the Council of Ministers and the European Parliament, or the effect of proposed institutional changes or EU enlargement on that distribution (e.g. Nurmi, 1997).

These power indices have not, however, been without their critics. Thus, Max Albert (2003) has argued that the theory of power indices 'should not […] be considered as part of political science', and further that '[v]iewed as a scientific theory, it […] can safely be ignored by political scientists' (2003, p. 1). The theory of power indices, Albert argues, is not a positive theory; that is, it does not have falsifiable implications. Rather, Albert suggests, the theory is either a non-empirical branch of probability theory or an unconvincing branch of political philosophy. In either case, the theory 'has no factual content and can therefore not be used for purposes of prediction or explanation' (2003, p. 1).

This is probably rather too harsh a critique, but it does bring out some important aspects of measures of inequality more generally, given the similarity in the nature of the indices in economics and political science. Essentially, these indices in themselves are primarily exercises in political philosophy. Their construction is not based on positive—that is, on empirically falsifiable—theory but on a set of normative assumptions and formal mathematical derivations from these assumptions. So, in the case of the most widely-used measure of inequality, the Gini coefficient, the measure involves the intellectually awkward possibility that rather different distributions of income can lead to the same numerical value. (This is the case, for example, when the Lorenz curves cross). Hence, a number of economists, such as Anthony Atkinson, have developed alternative measures which are explicitly weighted to give more importance to what is happening at different parts of the distribution. And Atkinson is quite explicit that these weights involve normative judgements.

The key point is that standard measures of inequality, whether one looks at the Gini coefficient, or the Theil coefficient, or the log deviation, are all based on aggregated individual data, and all involve normative judgements about how to weight different individuals. It would not be unreasonable to regard them in the same way as Max Albert regards the power indices in political science, as exercises in political philosophy and mathematics, not exercises in explanatory scientific theory.

To be sure, these indices, whether of income inequality or inequality in voting power, have been used in a great deal of subsequent empirical research. In the case of income inequality, they can be quite good predictors; recent research, for example, shows that more unequal societies tend to have higher (perceived) levels of corruption (Uslaner, 2008; You and Khagram, 2005). This finding should give us food for thought, given the increasing inequality which countries like Britain and the USA have seen in Since the late 1970s. However, a properly scientific approach to these indices would be to compare the explanatory power of the alternative mathematical versions, and of alternative weightings, and to select the version of the index which has the greatest scientific value in predicting a relevant outcome. However, there is no sign that this is happening in economics, while little if any use has been made of indices of voting power in political science for explanatory purposes. The lack of empirical explanatory work should make us very cautious about taking such indices too seriously as scientific tools, though they may be invaluable as normative tools.

It is no surprise, then, that many arguments against inequality are essentially normative arguments, focusing on issues of social justice. There is also, of course, a large literature focusing on the negative consequences of inequality, such as the way in which it may inhibit economic growth or reduce social cohesion, trust, or social mobility. An appreciable amount of this research, at least in sociology, is largely based on static comparisons between different countries and it is not always clear that increasing levels of inequality over time, such as the ones we have seen in Britain since 1980, inevitably lead to the alleged negative outcomes. Contrary to what one might have expected from the static cross-national comparisons, social trust seems to have remained relatively stable in

Britain, and crime has, in fact, declined over the last 20 years, despite increasing economic inequality.

Be this as it may, my main argument is that it is not so much the individual differences in income or wealth as the group-based ones which empirically are likely to be the major drivers of a range of adverse political outcomes such as political disturbances and conflict. So, if we are interested in the relationship between economic inequality and political outcomes, maybe we should be moving from individualistic treatments of inequality and power towards group-based ones. In other words, then, rather than extending individualistic models from economics to political science, might we not be better off moving in the opposite direction? Should we not complement the primarily individualistic approach of standard economics to the measurement of inequality and power with a group-based approach like that of C. Wright Mills?

I am not suggesting that individual inequalities should be completely ignored but, simply, that they are not likely to be sufficient for explaining many contemporary phenomena with which one might expect political science to be concerned. Let me give an example. Within the UK, people who are as old as I am will remember 'The Troubles' in Northern Ireland. Basically, Britain had a civil war for a period of about 20 years in Northern Ireland. (While official accounts never termed it a civil war, the death toll certainly reached the threshold that academic scholarship has taken to indicate a civil war.) While the historical causes of any conflict are bound to be complex, the troubles can, at least in part, be attributed to the long-standing economic and political inequalities between the Protestant and Catholic communities, between two communities whose members largely identified with their co-religionists: the Protestants identified with other Protestants; the Catholics with other Catholics. Catholics were systematically excluded from certain forms of economic power, of which one index was that the unemployment rates of Catholics were between 2.0 and 2.5 times as high as those of Protestants. This had remained true for a very substantial period and undoubtedly was due, at least in part, to various forms of discrimination, both direct and indirect discrimination. Similarly, the first-past-the-post electoral system, coupled with a degree of gerrymandering of constituency boundaries, led to the effective exclusion of Catholics from political power. Fair employment programmes, and power-sharing in politics, have made major contributions to the subsequent peace process.

If you approach these issues from an individualistic angle, however, you would probably find that overall economic inequality was little different (probably less) in Northern Ireland than it was in the rest of the UK at the time. And you would probably find that religious affiliation explained, at best, 10 % of the individual variation in income inequality or individual risks of unemployment in Northern Ireland, the remaining 90 % being due to individual differences. However, it was the 10 % that was group-based that drove the conflict. It is the group-based aspect of economic and political inequalities, then, that is particularly important for understanding conflict.

How are we to explain the way in which group-based differences dominate individual differences, at least in the explanation of political conflict? A good starting point is the social psychological concept and theory of social identity, developed around 40 years ago by Tajfel, Billig, Bundy, and Flament (1971) and J.C. Turner (1975). One of the key ideas is that of in-group preference and, correspondingly, out-group rejection. The theory provides a basis for understanding why prejudice and discrimination against members of out-groups remain so widespread, phenomena which economists have long struggled to explain and which, according to standard theory, should not occur in a perfect market of profit-maximising firms. To be sure, social identity is now, rather belatedly, coming to be incorporated into economic thinking (see, for example, Akerlof & Kranton, 2000; Darity, Mason, & Stewart, 2006; Davis, 2014), although it remains far outside the mainstream.

However, I suspect that social identity theory is not quite sufficient on its own to explain contemporary conflicts such as those in Northern Ireland. Another important explanatory idea is provided by W.G. Runciman's even older theory of fraternal relative deprivation (1966). The key idea in Runciman's work is that not only may people identify with those who share the same social identity, but they may also come to share a sense of grievance and injustice if they feel that their fellow group members are unfairly treated by those in economic or political authority. This sense of shared grievance or fraternal relative deprivation may still be felt, even if the individual himself or herself has not personally experienced discrimination or unemployment. The sense of outrage or grievance about the treatment of one's social group does not require that one has individually experienced ill-treatment. Runciman captures this sense through his use of the term 'fraternal'. And it is this fraternal sense of grievance over the treatment of one's group that can explain why, even if there is a great deal of individual variation in the extent of economic disadvantage experienced by, say, Catholics in Northern Ireland, the 10 % of the variation which is due to anti-Catholic discrimination can still be pivotal.

In the political sphere, then, a major mobilising force can be group solidarity coupled with shared feelings of grievance about the way in which members of one's group are treated. One key challenge in relating inequality to political conflict and mobilisation, then, is to understand the way in which individual differences are structured along lines of social identity communities. Individual differences alone, in the absence of social identities and senses of shared grievance, are unlikely to have much impact in the political sphere. The incentive to be a free-rider will see to that. Or, to take Hirschman's famous trilogy of exit, voice, and loyalty (Hirschman, 1970), the rational individualist is highly likely to choose exit; the choices of voice and loyalty are more likely where social identities are involved, voice being more likely where there is a sense of fraternal relative deprivation, loyalty where there is, say, a shared sense of national identity and belonging.

My argument, then, is that high levels of income inequality between individuals may not inevitably lead to political conflict. Individuals who are dissatisfied by their low position in the income distribution often have the option of exit: they can seek to emigrate for example, as many Britons historically did and, indeed, continue to do. Historical research might show that outward migration from Britain was at its lowest in the 1950s and 1960s when Britain had domestic full employment and low income inequality.

Purely individualistic accounts have difficulty with understanding voice, because of the free-rider problem which affects the provision of public goods (Olson, 1965). A shared sense of grievance or social injustice among members of excluded groups, such as the young people who have been particularly hard hit by the Great Recession and the subsequent austerity measures, is likely to be a major driver of vocal protest.

In conclusion, I feel we need an empirical research agenda which seems to understand the relationship between income (or wealth) inequality and collective political action, focusing not only on excluded groups, but also on the collective action engaged in by elites. This research agenda needs to investigate not just the correlations, but also the mechanisms which generate the collective action. It needs to take group-based explanations seriously, in the way advocated by George Akerlof, and not assume that a purely individualistic methodology will suffice.

References

Akerlof, G. A., & Kranton, R. E. (2000). Economics and identity. *Quarterly Journal of Economics, 115*, 715–753.

Akerlof, G. A., & Kranton, R. E. (2002). Identity and schooling: Some lessons for the economics of education. *Journal of Economic Literature, 40*(4), 1167–1201.

Albert, M. (2003). The voting power approach: Measurement without theory. *European Union Politics, 4*(3), 351–366.

Darity, W. A., Mason, P. L., & Stewart, J. B. (2006). The economics of identity: The origin and persistence of racial norms. *Journal of Economic Behavior and Organization, 60*, 283–305.

Davis, J. B. (2014). Stratification economics and identity economics. *Cambridge Journal of Economics.* (2015) 39 (5): 1215-1229.

Galbraith, J. K. (1998). *Created unequal: The crisis in American pay.* New York: Free Press.

Galbraith, J. K., Choi, J., Halbach, B., Malinowska, A., & Zhang, W. (2015). *A comparison of major world inequality data sets* (UTIP Working Paper 69). http://utip.gov.utexas.edu

Gelman, A., Katz, J., & Tuerlinckx, F. (2002). The mathematics and statistics of voting power. *Statistical Science, 17*(4), 420–435.

Hirschman, A. O. (1970). *Exit, voice and loyalty: Responses to decline in firms, organizations, and states.* Cambridge, MA: Harvard University Press.

Keynes, J. M. (1933). *Essays in persuasion.* London: Macmillan.

Khagram, 'A Comparative Study of Inequality and Corruption', American Sociological Review February 2005 vol. 70 no. 1 136–157.

Kuznets, S. (1955). Economic growth and income inequality. Presidential Address to the American Economic Association, *American Economic Review* Vol. 45, Issue 1, (March 1955), 1–28.

Mills, C. W. (1956). *The power elite*. New York: Oxford University Press.

Nurmi, H. (1997). The representation of voter groups in the European Parliament: A Penrose-Banzhaf index analysis. *Electoral Studies, 16,* 317–327.

Olson, M. J. (1965). *The logic of collective action: Public goods and the theory of groups*. Cambridge, MA: Harvard University Press.

Penrose, L. (1946). The elementary statistics of majority voting. *Journal of the Royal Statistical Society, 109*(1), 53–57.

Piketty, T. (2013). *Capital in the twenty-first century*. Cambridge: Harvard University Press.

Runciman, W. G. (1966). *Relative deprivation and social justice: A study of attitudes to social inequality in twentieth-century England*. London: Routledge/Kegan Paul.

Tajfel, H., Billig, M., Bundy, R., & Flament, C. (1971). Social categorization and intergroup behavior. *European Journal of Social Psychology, 1,* 149–178.

Turner, J. (1975). Social comparison and social identity. *European Journal of Social Psychology, 5,* 5–34.

Uslaner, E. M. (2008). *Corruption, inequality, and the rule of law: The bulging pocket makes the easy life*. Cambridge: Cambridge University Press.

Zhang, W. (2014). *Has China crossed the threshold of the Kuznets curve?* (UTIP Working Paper 67).

Index

CPI Antony Rowe
Chippenham, UK
2017-05-29 09:44